FOUND
A Story of Faith, Healing and Hope

Disclaimer

This book shares the personal journey of the author and is intended to offer encouragement and inspiration to others walking through faith, healing, and life's struggles. It is not intended to substitute for professional medical, psychological, or spiritual advice.

If you are experiencing emotional distress or mental health concerns, please seek support from a qualified healthcare professional or contact a helpline in your area.

The opinions expressed in this book are those of the author and do not represent any specific church, organisation, or denomination in an official capacity.

Copyright © 2025 Tanya Wood

All rights reserved.
No part of this publication may be reproduced, stored in a retrieval system, or transmitted in any form or by any means — electronic, mechanical, photocopying, recording, or otherwise — without the prior written permission of the author, except for brief quotations used in reviews, articles, or academic purposes.

Scripture quotations marked (NIV) are taken from The Holy Bible, New International Version®, NIV®. Copyright ©1973, 1978, 1984, 2011 by Biblica, Inc.® Used by permission. All rights reserved worldwide.

This book is a work of nonfiction. Some names or identifying details may have been changed to protect the privacy of individuals.

Published in Australia by Tanya Leigh Wood

ISBN: 978-1-7642114-1-3
Cover design by: Tanya Leigh Wood

Printed in Australia.

www.tanyaleighwood.com.au

FOUND

A Story of Faith, Healing and Hope

Acknowledgements

To my Heavenly Father —
To the One who found me before I ever thought to look. Thank You for not giving up on me. For seeing me in the middle of the mess, for whispering when the noise was too loud, for showing up in the small things, and for staying when I didn't know how to stay close. This book is only possible because You never let go.

To Jesus —
Thank You for rewriting my story with grace. For meeting me gently, walking me forward, and carrying me when I couldn't take another step. Thank You for setting the perfect example to follow.

To the Holy Spirit —
Thank You for guiding me through every word, prompting, nudging, comforting, and growing me through this process.

To my husband —
Thank you for your patience, support, and for letting me become who God is calling me to be, even when it looks unfamiliar. You've stood beside me through the ups and downs, and I'm grateful beyond words.

To my children —
You've been my greatest teachers and my biggest joys. I pray this journey points you toward Jesus — not just through my words, but through my life.

To my church family —
Thank you for embracing me, for encouraging my faith, and for being living examples of God's compassion and community. Your love changed me more than you'll ever know.

To my boss and friend —
Thank you for asking the question that changed everything, and for planting a seed that God would water and grow.

To every reader —
Thank you for opening these pages. If even one part of this book helps you feel seen, held, or drawn closer to God — then every tear, every prayer, every hard chapter has been worth it.

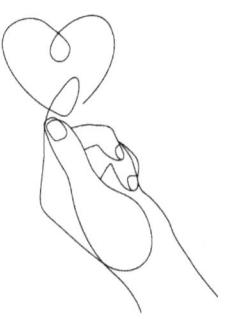

*"I wasn't seeking, I wasn't ready, I wasn't whole.
And still—He found me."*

— FOUND

Introduction

For the One Who Wonders if God Is Even Real

I didn't grow up with God.
I didn't know the Bible.
I didn't pray.
And to be honest? I wasn't even sure He existed.

It wasn't that I had turned away from Him—I had simply never known Him. God was a word I might've heard in passing, but He wasn't part of my world. Not someone I spoke to. Not someone I believed could talk back.

Then one day, a conversation with my boss unexpectedly turned toward faith. He invited me to church—and while I didn't have answers, or even much curiosity, something in me cracked open. I had a tired heart, a chaotic life, and a quiet sense that maybe… just maybe… *There was something more.*

That small invitation led to a very big shift.

I wasn't seeking, I wasn't ready, I wasn't whole. And still—He found me.

If you had told me five years ago that I'd be writing a book about God, I wouldn't have believed you. Back then, life felt like survival—one challenge after another, pain upon pain. I was overwhelmed and uncertain where my story was heading. But even then, something was stirring beneath it all.

A whisper in the noise. A knock I didn't yet know how to answer.

And then, *everything changed.*

It didn't happen all at once—no lightning bolts or dramatic turning points—but slowly, quietly, and deeply. I started reading Scripture. I began to ask questions. I watched. I listened. And somewhere along the way, I found Him—or maybe, more accurately, I realised He had already found me.

It was a pull I couldn't explain.
A conversation here.
A Bible verse there.
A moment in worship.
A hospital room.
A text at just the right time.

God started showing up—not in grand displays, but in the everyday moments.

In the brokenness. In the stillness. In the mess.

This book is a reflection of that journey.

It's not a neat, polished testimony.

It's raw and real—filled with stories of fear and faith, failure and healing, grief and joy. But through it all, one thing remains constant: *God never left.*

There were times I doubted.
Times I struggled.
Times I felt like giving up completely.
But every time, in one way or another, God met me. Not always how I expected—but always how I needed.

And so, I wrote this for the one who isn't sure.
For the one who's hurting, questioning, or curious. For the one who feels too far gone or too broken to be found.

My hope is that in these pages, you'll begin to see Him too—maybe not all at once, but in the slow unfolding of your own story.

I pray this book opens a door, like one was opened for me—that grows into a relationship with the God who sees you, loves you, and walks with you through it all.

I didn't find God by accident.
And it is not an accident you opened this book.

You don't need to have it all figured out.

You just need to open the door.

And walk through it.

Let's take this journey together—step by step, chapter by chapter—with eyes wide open to the God who's been there all along.

Because long before I knew His name...
I was already being found.

Contents

1. The Beginning I Didn't See Coming — 1
2. Before the Light — 9
3. Still so Green — 19
4. When One Heart Turns, Others Follows — 27
5. A Different Kind of Christmas — 37
6. The Month That Changed Everything — 47
7. Too Good Not to Share — 57
8. Where Faith Took Root — 67
9. Stepping Out in Faith — 77
10. When Prayers Turn Personal — 89
11. Touching His Cloak — 101
12. Grace for the Hard Days — 111
13. To Love and Let Go — 123
14. The Bookstore Breakthrough — 137
15. The Closeness that Saves — 153

16.	Miracles in the Mess	175
17.	Lighthouses in the Storm	185
18.	The Day I Said Yes	199

Epilogue: A Story Still Being Written	209
About the author	215
References	216
Appendix: Scripture References	220

*"Even when I didn't know how to believe,
God was pursuing my heart."*

— FOUND

Chapter One
THE BEGINNING I DIDN'T SEE COMING

It was the last day of June. I don't remember exactly what kind of day it was—probably cold, being the middle of winter in Australia—but I remember the fear.

Not the kind that brushes past you and disappears, but the kind that settles in your chest like a weight you can't shake off.

I stood outside the doors of my workplace, whole body trembling, knowing today was the day I had to tell my boss I was leaving, my heart was racing with a hundred what-ifs.

At the time, I was working part-time as a phlebotomist—what some jokingly call a vampire—and occasionally filled in as a medical receptionist at our local doctor's surgery. Just 15 or so hours a week.

I hadn't been there long, just under six months, but I genuinely loved the work. The people. The rhythm of the place. It gave me purpose.

Still, there was this heavy ache I couldn't ignore—the guilt of not contributing as much financially as I once had. That guilt can be relentless. It gnawed at the edges of my peace.

A week earlier, I'd gone for a promotion. I didn't get it. That stung more than I wanted to admit. I tried to shrug it off, brushing away the disappointment like lint on a sleeve.

"God obviously has other plans for me", I said nervously to my boss after I had verbally given him my notice.

Just a phrase. Just something to say to make the awkward moment feel less... final.

But as the words left my mouth, I caught myself. *Why did I say that?* I didn't even know if I believed it. I mean, I didn't think there wasn't a God—but I wasn't exactly convinced there was one either.

I suppose you could say I was agnostic. Suspended somewhere between belief and doubt, curiosity and indifference.

Still, that one little phrase—*"God has other plans"*—sparked something. A moment. A conversation. A door cracking open. My boss was a Christian, and what followed wasn't a sermon or a million questions, but a gentle, unassuming conversation that left me thinking that maybe I should pick up a Bible. Maybe it was the sincerity in his response. Or perhaps it was something deeper that was beginning to stir.

Later that day, after work, I was a mess.

On paper, I'd made the right choice. I'd already secured a new job with more hours and better pay. Logically, it made sense. We'd be in a better position financially. We could finally breathe a little easier.

But emotionally, I was wrecked. The second I walked out of that doctor's surgery, I felt it—that sickening knot of regret tightening in my stomach.

I couldn't stop crying.

Not just a tear or two. Full-body sobs. The kind where you gasp for air and can't form a complete sentence. I sat there, unravelling—a literal shipwreck, capsized in a sea of confusion and sadness.

Why was I so upset? Was it the people I was going to miss? The familiarity? The shift from team environments to working solo in an isolated office.

Maybe. But deep down, it felt like more than that. Like I'd just walked away from something I wasn't supposed to leave behind.

Even though it was the *"right"* decision, it didn't feel right.

That night, with red eyes and puffy cheeks, I poured it all out to my husband. He sat with me in my chaos—calm, steady, supportive. And in the middle of my breakdown, he encouraged me to do something that seemed completely irrational but entirely necessary.

"Message him" he said. *"Just see if it's not too late to change your mind."*

So, I did. Desperate and sobbing, I picked up my phone and messaged my boss. Not just asking—*begging*—for my job back. I was vulnerable, exposed and completely unfiltered. I laid my pride down and pleaded for him to take me back.

When I found out that they were not going to replace me because they realised that, technically, they didn't need me, my anxiety grew.

So, I wrote an email too. I listed every reason why I thought I was worth keeping. I laid everything bare. I don't usually go to such lengths, even when applying for jobs. Maybe that was why I didn't get the promotion.

But this? This wasn't about pride anymore. It felt like purpose. Like I needed to fight for something I didn't fully understand. The urge to return, to reclaim my earned vampire title, was way too strong to ignore.

And then came the waiting.

It was only a few days, but it felt like forever. My anxiety spiralled—what if they said no? What if I'd burned the bridge? What if I had to live with the consequences of a decision that felt so, so wrong?

But then... *he said yes.*

My boss agreed to take me back. No big ceremony, no fuss—just a simple, *"We'd love to have you back."*

I couldn't believe it. I had been completely unhinged—emotional, desperate, a total mess. But also—driven. Determined. Like something inside me had known all along that I needed to stay.

And it was in that messy, unglamorous moment that I made a quiet decision.

I'm going to give this whole God thing a try.

Because what was that feeling? That pull? That ache in my gut that refused to let go until I did something about it. Was it anxiety? Intuition? Or... was it God?

I didn't have the answers. But I couldn't deny the sense that something—or Someone—was drawing me toward a different path. A better one. Not easier. But right.

So I downloaded the Bible app. Just out of curiosity. YouVersion, if you want to look it up. It's free (I know, classic PR move—but seriously, no strings attached). It not only gives you access to the Bible in many different translations and languages, but it has a huge range of reading plans you can do by yourself or with friends.

I didn't know what I was searching for. I just knew that something had shifted. Something inside me was waking up.

Somehow, *even when I didn't know how to believe, God was pursuing my heart.*

And that was the beginning of something I couldn't have planned, predicted, or even prayed for.

> *"In their hearts humans plan their course, but the LORD establishes their steps"*
> *— Proverbs 16:9*

And that, my friends, was the beginning of my journey with God.

"The lights had shut off inside me, and the once-vibrant parts of my personality began to dim."

— FOUND

Chapter Two

BEFORE THE LIGHT

Let's backtrack a little—so you can get a sense of who Tanya *pre-God* was.

In my thirty-something years of life, I've been on a rollercoaster—a wild, unpredictable, and often bumpy ride. There were exhilarating highs and crushing lows, moments of laughter followed by waves of quiet despair. Sometimes the ride would stall unexpectedly, needing repairs before it could continue.

But after nearly 28 years of climbing mountains and trudging through valleys, my ride finally broke down. And I believed it was *beyond* repair this time.

Mentally, I was in a very dark place.

I couldn't see a way out. I felt hollow, like an empty shell of who I used to be. *The lights had shut off inside me, and the once-vibrant parts of my personality began to dim.* Slowly, I began to evacuate everyone off the ride—I shut down emotionally and socially. No one knew how long I'd be out of action, and to be honest, neither did I. I wasn't even sure I wanted to return.

And yet, through it all, *my husband stayed.*

He stayed when I was distant. He stayed when I was angry. He stayed when I barely spoke. He worked tirelessly to help repair the woman he married when he could've so easily walked away.

He didn't try to fix me with empty words or quick solutions. He just showed up—every single day. Steady, patient, strong.

He's the hardest-working man I've ever met, and without him, I don't know if I'd be here today, telling this story.

What I experienced was a *full-blown mental breakdown.*

It wasn't loud or dramatic. It didn't look like what people might expect. It crept in quietly, like a fog rolling across a field, clouding everything in my life until I couldn't see the path forward.

It hit the version of me that everyone thought had it all together: bubbly, positive, always-smiling Tanya. The Tanya who helped others, who laughed easily, and who got things done.

So, you can imagine the shock it must have been for those closest to me when I suddenly wasn't her anymore.

Despite the doctors, psychologists, and the ever-changing medication plans that tried to fix me, *it was my husband who carried me through the worst of it.*

Recovery was not quick, and it was far from straightforward. It wasn't a movie montage of progress—it was messy, inconsistent, and exhausting.

I often describe that season as being *stuck in a deep, dark hole.*

People would toss things down to try and help—ropes, ladders, advice—but none of it reached me. None of it worked. I was too far gone to grab hold.

One psychologist in particular tried to dredge up parts of my childhood I had long since buried. She cast out a fishing line into the murky waters of my past, hoping to hook onto something meaningful.

But every memory she tried to pull up only made the walls around me collapse further in. I had done everything I could to suppress the trauma of my younger years, and the more she prodded, *the harder it became to breathe.*

Maybe my past wasn't truly buried. Maybe it had been quietly leaking out of me all along—and this breakdown was the breaking point, *the flood*.

I didn't stay long with that psychologist. But I did take one thing from her, one piece of advice that ended up changing everything: *write it down*.

So, I did.

Not with the intention of ever publishing anything. Not even to share it with anyone. I wrote simply because I didn't know what else to do. I wrote to release the pain. I wrote to make sense of the chaos in my mind. I wrote to process things I hadn't let myself feel since I was a young girl.

Somehow, through the motion of pen on paper—or fingers on a keyboard—*I began to breathe again*.

Writing became my therapy. My anchor. My lifeline.

And little did I know, it would grow into something far more than an outlet. It would become a passion. It would become a calling. *It would become this story*.

And maybe, just maybe, it would become a way to help someone else open their heart to Jesus.

After being *"out of action"* for a while, and with my husband's relentless support and that one piece of advice tucked into my back pocket, *I slowly began to heal.*

One particular day stands out in my memory. My youngest son, Charlie—just shy of two years old—clung to me like never before. He wasn't usually the clingy type. He was chilled, independent, the kind of toddler who'd happily play on his own for hours.

But that day, he wouldn't let me go. If I stepped away, even for a moment, he'd sook and cry until I scooped him into my arms.

I can still see his little tear-filled eyes looking up at me, then melting into a smile the moment I held him.

That moment broke something open in me.

I had just finished writing about my teenage pregnancy—one of the hardest yet most defining experiences of my life. Surprisingly, it wasn't a traumatic memory to revisit. Instead, it reminded me how far I'd come as a woman, as a mother, and as a wife. And in that moment, holding my youngest child while reflecting on the journey that led me to him, I felt a shift inside.

It reminded me that *I was needed.*

That *I was loved.*

That just my presence was enough to light up his little world.

And slowly, the shell I had become began to fill back up—with hope, with warmth, with purpose.

I didn't want to go back to that dark place ever again. I knew I needed something to keep my motor running, something to ignite life back into me. So, one winter evening, sitting outside under a blanket of stars with my husband of eight years, we made a spontaneous decision.

We decided to buy a 4WD and a camper trailer.

And just like that, we packed up our entire life and hit the road—with our four children in tow.

Yes, four. Four beautiful, wild, hilarious little humans that we created together.

What an adventure it turned out to be.

Australia's landscape unfolded before us—the turquoise waters and vibrant coral of the Ningaloo Reef, the remote red cliffs and pearl-white sands of Cape Leveque, the endless stretch of the Nullarbor Plain where the sky meets the earth in silence, the powdery beaches and crystal coves of Esperance, and the starry skies that stretched further than I ever imagined. We weren't just sightseeing. We were healing. We were reconnecting. We were becoming.

But it wasn't always easy. There were moments I longed for stability. Times I missed my mum, my sister, our friends and families. I'd find myself craving a quiet moment alone, something nearly impossible to come by in a camper full of kids. And of course, finances were tight. We were living simply, often scraping by.

There were nights I lay awake questioning our decision. Wondering if we should turn back.

But somewhere along the way—after the dust, the detours, and the difficult days—*we found our rhythm.*

We learnt how to breathe again. We figured out how to pause when we needed to. To slow down. To live differently. And by the time our original twelve-month plan ended, none of us were ready to stop.

That one year gradually stretched into *two and a half.*

Two and a half years of driving, laughing, arguing, exploring, growing. *An unexpected journey I will never forget.*

Eventually, the road led us to a quiet little country town—on the *complete opposite side of the country* from where we began. In the very state we spent the most time in and fell in love with.

We bought a shabby old fixer-upper on a block of acreage within a welcoming community, we found jobs that gave us purpose and began building a life we genuinely enjoyed.

And it was there—*right there*—in that quiet, unlikely place...

that *I opened my heart to God.*

> *"He lifted me out of the slimy pit, out of the mud and mire; he set my feet on a rock and gave me a firm place to stand." — Psalm 40:2*

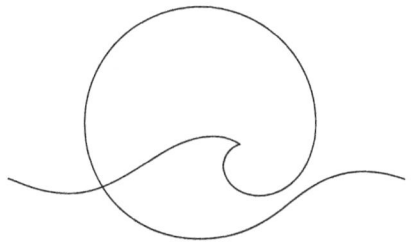

"It felt overwhelming, like I'd jumped into the deep end without knowing how to swim."

— FOUND

Chapter Three
STILL SO GREEN

A few months passed after I first opened the Bible.

I was slow to start—this was all so new.

Scary. Weird. Unknown.

And during that time, life didn't exactly go smoothly. I went through some pretty hard trials—really hard ones. Yet somehow, I found myself standing in October.

That's when my boss mentioned something called *Happy Holiday Club*—an annual church holiday program for kids. Bible stories, arts and crafts, fun worship music, skits, games... the kids loved it.

But no one loved it more than Emileigh, my second youngest. She came home absolutely buzzing, singing the songs at the top of her lungs and retelling the stories with so much joy. *She was hooked.*

After I told my boss how much she had enjoyed it, he invited us to something called *Sabbath School,* held every Saturday morning.

Sabbath School? Church on a Saturday?

What even was the Sabbath?

I had no idea what kind of religious group I'd been exposed to. That's how green I was. My only real exposure to religion had been tagging along to a Catholic church with a friend about twenty years ago—and a brief Christian phase my brother went through in his late teens. That was it.

Still, one Saturday morning in late October, I decided to give it a go—for Emileigh's sake mostly. She was so excited, like a kid on Christmas morning. I figured, at the very least, it would be a special mother-daughter thing. The other kids weren't too fussed, but she couldn't wait.

So, what is Sabbath School?

It's kind of like Sunday School, so I've been told—but on Saturdays. Everyone gathers together at first for prayer, singing, a mission story, and sometimes even a quiz. Then we split off into smaller age-based groups for Bible study. There are bible studies for the younger kids, youth, and adults—and different church members take turns leading them.

I chose to go with Emileigh's group. The younger kids. I felt like one of them—so green that even they knew more than I did about this amazing God.

They told age-appropriate Bible stories, sometimes acted them out (which was adorable), and always had a fun activity or craft at the end. I actually really enjoyed it. Especially the word searches! Though I did quickly learn that I'm terrible at cutting out shapes. I made a mental note to work on that particular skill—because hey, you never know when precise scissor skills might come in handy.

Week after week, we kept going back. And my curiosity just kept growing.

At the time, I'd started exploring the Bible more, I chose to start at the very start, Genesis. Some heavy stuff in there—honestly, most of it didn't make a lot of sense to me. *It felt overwhelming, like I'd jumped into the deep end without knowing how to swim.*

Looking back, I probably should have started with the Gospels. They're filled with the life and words of Jesus—so personal, so full of love and grace. The Gospels meet you where you are, and I think that's what I really needed at that moment: *to meet Jesus first*. To understand His heart before trying to wrap my head around genealogies, ancient laws, or worldwide floods.

Eventually, I went to my boss and said, *"I think I'm ready to join the adult group."*

"You will seek me and find me when you seek me with all your heart." — Jeremiah 29:13

I needed guidance. I wanted to understand more. I wanted to seek Him more. With all of my heart.

I remember sitting in the church Bible study group for the first time, surrounded by adults, listening as they spoke about the lesson with such ease and confidence. Meanwhile, I sat quietly, stumbling over my own thoughts, unsure if I was even grasping anything at all.

Reading the Bible and following the discussions felt overwhelming at first—so many names, so much history, and far more questions than answers. But I was hungry for truth. And even in my lack of knowledge, I knew that God saw my heart.

That's when I really began to invest in this journey.

Each Sabbath, I kept showing up, still sitting with the adults, still unsure, but slowly beginning to understand bits and pieces. I still had my floaties on, but I was learning how to swim. And slowly, I started to feel like I belonged.

That's also when I met Mr. Hester—an elderly gentleman whose quiet faith left a lasting impression on me. He shared some of his own journey with me, how he found comfort in God, and how Christ had been his anchor through life's storms.

The next Sabbath, he handed me an old, worn-out Bible.

"Here, kid," he said. *"Since your generation only knows how to use phones, here's a real Bible."*

He liked to tease me about still reading the Bible on my phone. But I could tell, underneath the jokes, he was thrilled *I was reading it at all.*

He also gave me a book to read—*One Miracle After Another* by Greg Budd. "Some light reading," he added with a smirk.

That book—about the life of Pastor Pavel Goia—sat untouched on my bedside table for weeks. I kept telling myself I didn't have time, when really, I just wasn't making time. A habit I'm still working on.

Eventually, I picked it up. And I couldn't put it down.

Pavel's story was one of absolute trust in God—miracle after miracle unfolding because of his unwavering faith. That book became my first Christian read. It will forever hold a special place in my heart.

Funny enough, a few months later, I found out that Pastor Pavel Goia himself would be speaking at Easter Camp. *Yes, Easter Camp!* But let's not jump ahead—we're still in November.

By this point, I'd experienced Sabbath School, taken the plunge into the adult Bible study group, and started reading some eye-opening Scripture in both the Old and New Testaments. I had questions—a lot of them.

Thankfully, my boss and his wife graciously offered to answer them. I called it *"question time"*—a safe space where I could ask anything, no matter how simple or complicated. I was trying to soak up as much information as I could.

> *"Ask and it will be given to you; seek and you will find; knock and the door will be opened to you"*
> *— Matthew 7:7*

One of the things that absolutely blew my mind. That God, Jesus, and the Holy Spirit are one.

They're often referred to as the Godhead—or the Trinity. Three-in-one.

How had I never known this? Maybe I'd heard it before but never understood it. Either way, it fascinated me.

God is Father, Son, and Spirit. Three persons, one divine nature.

And just when I thought I couldn't be more amazed...

Something else happened next—something unexpected, *something that made my heart even fuller.*

Chapter Four
WHEN ONE HEART TURNS, OTHERS FOLLOWS

One Sabbath afternoon, after church had finished and the buzz of the service had settled, my husband sat quietly beside me when I arrived home. Then, without warning, he asked a question that caught me completely off guard:

"Are you going to keep exploring this God stuff?"

His voice was calm but sincere, like he was searching for something real.

"Heck yes!" I replied without hesitation—my heart already full of a growing certainty.

It wasn't just a passing interest anymore. This wasn't something I was dabbling in or checking off a list. It was becoming my life.

He could see it—the change within me, something real, something rooted deep inside. I wasn't simply going through the motions. I was growing. And he noticed.

His curiosity was obvious. Maybe a bit of confusion too. Why was I so committed to something I'd only just begun to explore? How could something I hadn't even believed in six months earlier now be the centre of my world?

I didn't have a perfect answer for him. Honestly, I was still figuring it out myself. But one thing was clear: *something had awakened in me.* And I didn't want to go back to sleep.

I had found hope. Peace. Purpose. A new rhythm for my life. And I was determined to keep going, to keep growing, and to reflect Jesus in everything I did.

And apparently... I had been. Because then came the words I never expected to hear:

"I think we should start going to church together as a family."

I could have cried. And I think I did.

Here was my husband—ready to explore his own faith, to understand the love and joy he saw in me.

The thought of our whole family walking this path together filled me with a kind of hope I hadn't dared to imagine before. Maybe, just maybe, they could all experience God's big, unshakable love too.

"See what great love the Father has lavished on us, that we should be called children of God! And that is what we are! The reason the world does not know us is that it did not know him." — 1 John 3:1

What I didn't realise until that moment was just how much exposure to religion Chris actually had. He could even recite the *Lord's Prayer*—which honestly shocked me. And I found out that his mother had even taught Sunday school when she was younger.

But knowing Scripture wasn't the same as truly knowing God. Chris still wasn't sure what he believed yet—but he was open. And that openness was all I needed.

What we both had yet to fully understand were the unique beliefs of the Seventh-day Adventist Church. This was when I started to dive deeper into the Sabbath.

In the Bible, it's clear that God created the world in six days and rested on the seventh, setting it apart as holy. This day of rest, reflection, and worship is called the Sabbath and is the fourth commandment.

I was curious—why do most Christian groups worship on Sunday, the first day of the week, instead of Saturday, the original Sabbath?

I learned that many observe Sunday in honour of Jesus' resurrection, which is believed to have occurred on Sunday. However, Seventh-day Adventists continue to observe the Sabbath from sunset Friday to sunset Saturday, following the biblical pattern established in creation and affirmed in the Ten Commandments.

Ellen G. White, a writer and founding figure in the Adventist movement, once wrote:

> "Because He had rested upon the Sabbath, 'God blessed the seventh day, and sanctified it'—set it apart to a holy use. He gave it to Adam as a day of rest. It was a memorial of the work of creation, and thus a sign of God's power and His love." — Ellen G. White, Patriarchs and Prophets, p. 48.

As I explored further, I began to realise that while the day of worship has significance, the heart behind our worship matters even more.

It's not just about marking a calendar—it's about giving God our full attention, devotion, and surrender. Whether it's Saturday or Sunday, what truly matters is that we worship Him with sincerity, not just once a week, but in the way we live every single day.

True worship is a lifestyle—one that honours God continually, with our thoughts, our actions, and our hearts fully turned toward Him.

So, the following Sabbath, our whole family went to church together—me, my husband, and our four children.

It was special in a way I can't quite put into words.

Even though the older two groaned—Chloe sneaking glances at the clock every five minutes, Logan nudging me to say he was bored—and the youngest, Charlie, clearly had ants—or maybe worms—in his pants, however Emileigh's joy was contagious. Her little face lit up just seeing us all together. It made my heart swell with hope and gratitude.

I prayed quietly that day:

Lord, help this bring us closer together—not just as a family, but as Yours.

The very next day, we had another one of our *"question time"* chats with my boss and his wife—only this time, Chris joined in. It was an open, safe space for him to ask anything, no matter how awkward or hard. And he did.

Chris is a thinker and a realist. He needs evidence. He's not much of a reader though. That made things tricky—how do you build faith if you don't dive into the Bible? But that didn't make it impossible. *Nothing is impossible with God.*

> "With man this is impossible, but with God all things are possible." — Matthew 19:26

We were recommended a movie called *The Case for Christ*. It's based on the real-life story of journalist Lee Strobel, who set out to try and disprove Christianity after his wife found faith. It felt fitting—me growing in faith, and Chris, while not trying to disprove, still figuring it all out.

The Case for Christ is also a published book if you're more of a reader—even a version for kids is available.

As I continued to walk this path, learning more about who God is and what Jesus has done, something else started bubbling up inside me—Insecurity.

The more I learned about how holy, perfect, and loving God is, the more I questioned whether I was truly worthy of that love.

The memories I'd buried deep began to resurface. I remembered the pain of being abandoned by my earthly father after my parents' divorce. I remembered the things that happened to me that should never happen to anyone. I remembered becoming a mother at sixteen and the judgment that came with it. I remembered the ache of feeling like I had to prove myself to the world—and to myself.

I'd worked so hard to build a life I could be proud of. I left school in Year 9 but still managed to provide for my family. I poured everything into being a good wife and mother. But beneath it all, I was driven by fear of failure—a quiet, relentless pressure to prove I wasn't a mistake.

So, when I came to know God, *I carried that same pressure into my faith.*

I thought I had to earn His love. Deserve His grace. Measure up.

But God began gently peeling that away.

Through Scripture. Through songs. Through the kindness of people that He placed in my life.

One verse, in particular, became an anchor for me:

> *"As for God, his way is perfect: The LORD's word is flawless; he shields all who take refuge in him."*
> *— Psalm 18:30*

God never asked me to be perfect. He only asked me to trust Him. *To take refuge in Him.*

I didn't need to perform for His affection. *I already had it.*

That truth is still sinking in.

But day by day, I'm learning that my worth isn't found in my past, my performance, or my productivity—it's found in *being His.* In being known. Loved. Chosen.

This part of the journey wasn't just about me finding faith—it was about realising that *when one heart turns to Jesus, it often creates a ripple effect.*

I didn't need to preach to my husband. I just needed to live it. To be changed. To reflect Jesus, even in my mess.

And somehow, through that…

Chris began to follow.

Not me. *But the One I'm following.*

*"It felt as though God had gathered everyone—
family, friends, those he loved—into one place
to grieve side by side. It was heartbreaking,
but also sacred."*

— FOUND

Chapter Five
A Different Kind of Christmas

Before I knew it, Christmas had arrived again.

For as long as I could remember, Christmas was always about quality time—being surrounded by family, indulging in good food, and the excitement of presents piled under the tree. As a child, it felt magical, wrapped in the warmth of traditions that seemed to stretch back forever.

I remember how Mum would stay up late on Christmas Eve, meticulously wrapping each gift with care and sneaking them under the tree once we'd all gone to bed. She'd always use different wrapping paper for the *"Santa presents"* just to make it believable. We'd wake up to find new piles of mystery gifts, tagged in handwriting that definitely didn't belong to her—but we pretended anyway.

We wanted to believe.

I think I was around ten or eleven when I finally pieced it together—that the magical North Pole visitors were really just Mum and Dad, playing their parts so we could hold on to the wonder a little longer.

But knowing the truth didn't take the magic away. If anything, it made it more meaningful.

Christmas mornings in our house were chaotic in the best way. We'd wake up at the crack of dawn, messy-haired and bleary-eyed—mine always looked like I'd been struck by lightning in my sleep.

Mum would already have the camera ready, capturing every unwrapping moment. Dad, with his video camera—I don't remember when he got that gadget. I do remember he only really brought it out for special occasions: birthdays, holidays, milestones. Those moments when everything felt whole.

After the thrill of tearing open presents, we'd get dressed up—meticulously, as if preparing for a grand event. Christmas was the one time of year Mum and Dad cared deeply about appearances. We'd be on our best behaviour, our outfits pristine, as we headed to my father's side of the family.

Their standards always felt a little out of reach to me. As a kid, I saw them as polished, refined—like they had everything together. Their homes were spacious and beautifully kept, every detail in place, and they carried themselves with a kind of grace I didn't fully understand yet. Looking back, it makes sense why Mum always wanted us to look our best before those visits, like we were walking into a display home inspection.

There was definitely a sense of pressure to present well, but it wasn't all uncomfortable. I did appreciate the warmth and attention—how they'd light up when they saw us, commenting on how much we'd grown.

"My, how you've grown!" they'd say, as if a whole year hadn't passed since the last time. I'd smile, say thank you, and do my best to behave.

But even as I felt their kindness, I also felt the tug of home—where we could kick off our shoes, where toys were scattered, and laughter was a little louder. Where everything felt less picture-perfect, but more *us*.

My nan was different. We saw her more often, and with her, I never had to pretend. She loved us just as we were. Although dirt under our fingernails seemed to be a major bother.

My pop, on the other hand, I remember only faintly. He passed away just before I turned seven. I'm told he was a quiet man, a painter by trade, who had served in World War II.

He and Nan had eight children—my dad was the baby of the family. I was born when most of my cousins were entering adulthood, so family gatherings often felt like I was a quiet observer in a sea of adults.

When Nan died in 2022, she left behind a massive family—four generations and counting. These days, I don't have much to do with them. Aside from the occasional scroll through social media, I have lost touch with all of them.

But Boxing Day? That was always my favourite. It belonged to Mum's side of the family—chaotic, relaxed, and overflowing with love. A tradition still alive today.

My pop—her dad—would play Santa, throwing on a festive hat and calling us up one by one to hand out gifts. He didn't have the traditional white beard or round belly, but his huge smile and infectious joy lit up every room he entered.

Mum was the second eldest of four siblings. Her mother—my nan—lost her battle with breast cancer before I was even born, leaving behind not just her children and grandchildren, but a grieving husband.

Their love story was unusual. As teenagers, Mum's parents knew each other but drifted apart—until years later, when Pop ended up in prison and Nan became his pen pal.

When he was released, they reunited, moved around, had kids, and finally settled in a humble housing commission home, spending the next 14 years together in it. It wasn't much, but it was always full of love.

That home was a sanctuary—not just for them, but for nieces, nephews, friends, and anyone who needed a place to belong. It was always loud, always alive, always home.

In 2019, we said goodbye to that home; it was hard. But losing Pop unexpectedly that year was something else entirely. We have lost people before, but that loss hit differently.

He wasn't just family; *he was the heart of it.*

For as long as I could remember, every year we gathered at a special place before summer hit—a big house by a lake where family and friends, near and far, reunited. It wasn't just a holiday. It was tradition, connection, love.

And no one looked forward to it more than Pop. It was his favourite place.

But that year, on the way to that very place, our amazing Pop took his final breath. *It felt as though God had gathered everyone—family, friends, those he loved—into one place to grieve side by side. It was heartbreaking, but also sacred.*

We cried. We laughed. We shared stories. We held each other up through the heaviness.

I still wish he'd made it just one more time. To watch one more sunset over the lake, share one more loud and messy family dinner, pose for one more group photo surrounded by those who adored him.

Though I've since moved far away—those memories still warm my heart. I cherish them deeply.

But this Christmas... this one was different.

We were on the other side of the country. No big family gatherings. No familiar traditions. No cousins clamouring for attention. No Santa hat on Pop's head.

And yet—it meant more than ever before.

Because now, I understood what Christmas was truly about.

For the first time, I celebrated Christmas not just as a holiday, but as the birth of Jesus—the One who came to save us, who offers eternal life.

I'd always known about Christmas, *but now I knew Jesus.*

This verse echoed in my heart throughout the season:

"For God so loved the world that he gave his one and only Son, that whoever believes in him shall not perish but have eternal life." – John 3:16

Christmas Eve that year fell on Sabbath, and our church held a special program to celebrate the birth of Jesus—our Lord, our Saviour, the Prince of Peace. The One who brings joy, hope, and love to all.

This wasn't just a story—it was my story. My rescue. My reason for joy.

Sitting there in the pews, my heart overflowed. It was the most emotional Christmas I had ever experienced—not because of what was under the tree, but because of what had taken root in my heart.

It was around this time that I began to understand something deeply important: *God is love.*

Not just that He has love, but that *He is love.* The very reason I could love—my family, my friends, even myself again—was because He loved me first.

I felt like I was back at school, learning lessons I wish someone had taught me when I was younger, lost in a sea of self-doubt.

Now I knew: every ounce of love I had ever given or received came from Him.

> *"And so we know and rely on the love God has for us. God is love. Whoever lives in love lives in God, and God in them." — 1 John 4:16*

That kind of love changed me.

It made me love harder. It made me see others differently.

It gave new meaning to the memories, the traditions, even the losses.

Looking back now, I'm overwhelmed with gratitude—for the God who waited patiently, for the people who loved fiercely, and for the grace that opened a door wide enough for me to walk through.

And now, Christmas will never be the same again.

"When fear told me to panic, prayer taught me to breathe. In the middle of the unknown, I held onto God like never before."

— FOUND

Chapter Six

THE MONTH THAT CHANGED EVERYTHING

The new year had arrived. By mid-January, Brenna—my boss's daughter—invited me to join a Bible buddies' group through the YouVersion app.

The group was made up of Christian women around my age, all in different seasons of life but walking the same road of faith. Our first study was titled *Knowing God's Heart*.

Each day, we would read a short devotional, reflect on Scripture, and then share our thoughts in the group chat. I found myself excited to open the app each morning, curious about what God would speak to me that day.

And just like that, I was opening my Bible daily—not out of duty, but desire.

"Taste and see that the LORD is good; blessed is the one who takes refuge in him." — Psalm 34:8

The more time I spent in Scripture, the more natural prayer started to become. But if I'm honest, personal prayer was a bit intimidating at first. I remember thinking, how do I do this? Am I doing it right? Is there a formula I'm missing?

Everyone kept saying, *"Just talk to God. He's always listening"* but my overthinking brain wasn't convinced. So, instead of opening the Bible for guidance (which now feels ironic), I turned to Google.

The first tip I found? Find a quiet place where you can focus.

Easier said than done in a house full of kids who still acted like we lived in a caravan.

But I tried. I started carving out time in the mornings, right after Chris left for work and just before the chaos of little footsteps filled the house. I'd kneel beside my bed, fingers laced, head bowed.

At first, my prayers were short and awkward: *"God, thank You. I'm grateful. Please forgive me. And... thank You again. Amen."*

It didn't feel polished. But it was real.

Prayer, I was learning, wasn't about saying all the right things. It was about a relationship. About connection.

It was less about the structure and more about surrender. And gradually, I stopped trying to impress God and started talking to Him.

"And my God will meet all your needs according to the riches of his glory in Christ Jesus."
— Philippians 4:19

That lesson—trust—was about to be tested.

Back in late 2014, Chris had been diagnosed with cancer. It was an 18-month battle, and by God's grace, he came out the other side. But the trauma never really left us. It lingered in the background like a shadow that never fully disappeared.

So when Chris became unwell again in January, panic instantly crept in. He was exhausted all the time, sometimes pulling over just to rest during long work trips. I urged him repeatedly to see a doctor, but he hesitated. I knew why—he was scared too.

Eventually, he went for a checkup. Routine blood tests followed.

Then came the Sunday night phone call.

Those are never good.

His iron levels were undetectable. The doctor sounded concerned. Chris needed an urgent iron infusion and more tests to find out what was going on.

When his CT scan came back, I read the report and saw a single line that shattered me: *"PET scan recommended to rule out metastases."*

That word. *Metastases*. My chest tightened. I felt sick. It was like being thrown back into 2014 with the breath knocked out of me. I couldn't stop shaking. Fear had me in its grip.

That Sabbath, just before Chris's PET scan, my boss asked if the church could pray for him. I said yes without hesitation. I needed every voice I could gather crying out to God.

As people formed into small prayer groups that morning, I sat alone at first, trying not to cry. But as the prayers rose, so did the emotion. I broke. Completely.

My boss and his wife pulled me into their group, wrapped me in prayer, and for the first time, I felt the undeniable presence of the Holy Spirit.

It was overwhelming. Comforting. Holy.

A room full of people, many of whom barely knew Chris, praying fervently for his healing.

That, to me, was a glimpse of heaven. A glimpse of the heart of Jesus.

> *"Those who know your name trust in you, for you, LORD, have never forsaken those who seek you."*
> *— Psalm 9:10*

That afternoon, I went home and poured out everything to God. The fear. The hope. The questions. The surrender. And for the first time, I truly said it and meant it: *"Your will be done."*

The week crawled by. Every day, I prayed the same thing: *"Please, God, let it not be cancer. But Your will, not mine."*

When fear told me to panic, prayer taught me to breathe. In the middle of the unknown, I held onto God like never before.

Some days, the tears came fast. Some days I felt strong. But each day, I felt God near. I felt a peace that made no sense given the storm I was in.

And then came the call.

It wasn't cancer.

I cried—hard. Not just out of relief, but out of pure, reverent gratitude. God had carried me through the waiting. He had comforted me in the unknown. He had reminded me that faith is not just for the outcome—it's for the journey.

But the month wasn't done with us yet.

The very next Sabbath, Chris called me during Bible study. He never does that. I stepped outside to answer.

"Dolly's been bitten by a snake" he said, panic in his voice.

Dolly. Our Border Collie. Our fifth baby.

We rushed her to the vet—35 agonising kilometres away. Every minute felt like an eternity. The blood test confirmed our fear: snake venom.

I prayed hard. So did the church. And after six long hours, one enormous bill, and a lot of tears later—*Dolly survived.*

When I shared the news, my boss sent a message that stayed with me: *"He hears our prayers, even for a pet dog in the back blocks of a not very notable hot dusty town"*

And I believe that. I really do. Because that day, once again, God showed me that nothing is too small for His attention—not even a beloved pet and the people who love her.

> *"I will remember the deeds of the LORD; yes, I will remember your miracles of long ago."*
> *— Psalm 77:11*

February became the month that changed everything.

It was the month I learnt what it meant to truly trust. To pray without conditions. To give thanks in advance. To believe even when fear tried to crush my spirit.

It was the month I saw God show up—in comfort, in peace, in healing, and community.

It was the month I saw faith carried not just in quiet moments alone but in the hands and hearts of others. The church didn't just pray—they carried me. They reminded me what it meant to be part of the body of Christ.

It was the month I discovered that prayer is more than asking—it's worship. It's gratitude. It's a posture of surrender. It's a sacred dialogue where trust grows and hearts are changed. It's where the impossible becomes possible, not because we always get the answer we want, but because we come to know the One who holds every answer in His hands.

I no longer see prayer as a last resort. I see it as the lifeline it truly is.

It was the month that taught me that miracles come in many forms—not just in dramatic healings or unexpected breakthroughs, but in the peace that steadies your breath in the middle of the unknown, in the quiet assurance that God is near even when the waiting feels unbearable.

I learnt that the Holy Spirit speaks in whispers and waves. In the silence between sobs. In the voice of a friend. In the words of Scripture that suddenly feel alive.

Most of all, I learnt that when life unravels, *God doesn't.*

> *"Our Father in heaven, hallowed be your name, your kingdom come, your will be done, on earth as it is in heaven." — Matthew 6:9-10*

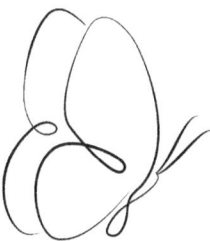

*"The butterfly does not fear change.
It embraces it, trusting in the
Creator's plan."*

— FOUND

Chapter Seven
Too Good Not to Share

March arrived quietly, but it brought with it something significant.

On the first Sabbath of the month, I met Pastor T—a visiting pastor from the city who occasionally came to share a message with our small church community. There was something steady and genuine about him. As he preached, his passion for the gospel came through in every word.

He spoke with such clarity and compassion that even the verses I'd heard before seemed to breathe in a new way. His presence was both calming and deeply stirring, leaving a quiet impact I couldn't quite explain.

After the service, we shared a basket lunch, and I had the chance to sit with him and talk more personally. I opened up about my story—where I'd come from, the unexpected turns that led me to faith, and how God had become undeniably real to me.

He listened with genuine interest, nodding thoughtfully, and offered quiet, wise encouragement that made me feel both heard and supported.

What stayed with me most was a simple but powerful truth that surfaced in our conversation: when Jesus becomes real in your life, it changes you. And when He changes you, you can't help but want others to know Him too.

I had already begun to feel that pull.

By now, I had seen God move in my life. I had felt the Holy Spirit stir something inside me. I had begun to understand who Jesus is—not just as a figure in history, but as a living Saviour. And that understanding sparked a new desire: I didn't want to just learn about Jesus—I wanted to become more like Him.

I wanted to share Him with the world.

That longing led me back to a topic we had explored in our online Bible study group—*the Fruit of the Spirit*. I pulled the plan back up in the YouVersion app and committed to revisiting each aspect: *love, joy, peace, patience, kindness, goodness, faithfulness, gentleness, and self-control.*

Each one felt beautiful. But each one felt out of reach.

I saw how far I had to go—how my patience wore thin when life felt too loud or chaotic, how gentleness sometimes gave way to sharpness when I was overwhelmed. But I wasn't discouraged. I was hungry for growth.

At the end of one of the devotionals, a question lingered: *"Are you longing to bear this fruit of the Spirit?"*

My answer was a quiet but certain yes.

> *"But the fruit of the Spirit is love, joy, peace, forbearance, kindness, goodness, faithfulness, gentleness and self-control." — Galatians 5:22-23*

So I began to pause more often—especially in the hard moments—and ask: *What would Jesus do here?*

It sounds simple. Maybe even cliché. But it began to work.

My reactions softened. My perspective began to shift. And little by little, peace began to take root in my everyday life. Not a perfect peace, but a growing one.

And through it all, God kept blessing me with friendships that nourished my soul.

On one Sabbath morning, I walked into church alone. A few of the women from our online Bible study were there in person—women I only knew by name until that day.

Brenna introduced us. One of them, Emily, smiled and invited me to sit beside her. Before the service began, we were hunched over a scrap piece of paper, playing Dots and Boxes—a game they all knew from childhood. We giggled like teenagers.

In those few minutes, something shifted. I didn't feel like a newcomer anymore. I felt known. Like these women had always been a part of my life.

That day marked the beginning of beautiful, Christ-centred friendships with Brenna, Kim, and Emily. They became a gift in my life, each one unique, each one intentional. Through them, I saw how community is part of God's design.

I didn't realise how much I needed women like them until God brought them into my world—women who would pray with me, laugh with me, and walk with me.

The joy we shared didn't just come from common interests—it came from shared purpose, from the unity that blossoms when hearts are turned toward Jesus.

We didn't have to perform or pretend. We could be real. Honest. Vulnerable. And through that kind of friendship, I saw Jesus more clearly.

The following month, on the first Sabbath of April, I experienced my first Communion Service.

I had been gently prepared for it by my boss, but nothing could have fully prepared me for the emotions that came with participating.

We began with what is called the Ordinance of Humility: *the foot-washing ceremony.*

It's based on the act Jesus did at the Last Supper—kneeling and washing the disciples' feet.

It was an act usually done by servants, yet Jesus did it to show the full extent of His love and humility.

At first, I felt nervous. My feet, still stained red from the pindan from our travels up north, felt unworthy of such honour. But when little Rach asked to wash my feet, something softened in me.

As I knelt and gently washed her feet, and as she washed mine, I felt something shift inside. The act was simple, but sacred.

I understood then that greatness in God's Kingdom comes through service.

> *"I am the bread of life."*
> *— John 6:48*

Next came: *the Lord's Supper.*

We broke the unleavened bread, remembering the body of Jesus broken for us.

We sipped the grape juice, a symbol of His blood poured out for our sins.

It was quiet. Personal. Holy. A moment of reflection and gratitude. A sacred space to recommit our lives to the One who gave everything.

> *"This is my blood of the covenant, which is poured out for many for the forgiveness of sins."*
> *— Matthew 26:28*

Together, as a church family, we honoured His sacrifice. And I left that service changed. Renewed. Humbled. More in love with Jesus than ever.

But with that love came a deeper awareness that it was time to let go of who I used to be.

The butterfly does not fear change. It embraces it, trusting in the Creator's plan.

Transformation takes time. You don't just wake up and become a butterfly. There's a process. A hidden work. A stillness. A quiet surrender. And I realised I had entered that very chrysalis months earlier—when I said an unspoken yes to that first conversation with my boss. That was the moment God began something new in me.

Now, I could feel it. A stirring. A shedding of the old. A becoming.

The caterpillar was the girl I used to be—moving slowly through life, surviving, striving, unaware of what she could become.

The chrysalis was where God met me—in the darkness, in the quiet, in the in-between, where everything familiar was being undone.

And the butterfly? That was the new creation He was forming. Not perfect. But lighter. Freer. His.

I began to see my life as a testimony still being written. Every page turned revealed more of His grace, more of His mercy, more of His fingerprints in my life.

I didn't have all the answers, and I wasn't done growing. But I knew I wasn't who I used to be.

When the gospel changes you, it won't stay quiet. It will echo in the way you live, speak, and love.

I couldn't keep it to myself. What God had done in me was too good, too life-changing, not to share. Day by day, that desire only grew stronger.

I started writing more—pouring out prayers in my journal, capturing little moments, telling stories that traced the fingerprints of God on my life.

I felt Him gently urging me:

Use your words. Speak life. Reflect My love in the everyday.

And that's when I realised—this journey was never meant to stay private. It was personal, yes, but not just for me.

It was for the ones still wandering, still aching, still wondering if they mattered at all. If I could speak one thing to them, it would be this: *You do.* More than you know.

> "Therefore, if anyone is in Christ, the new creation has come: The old has gone, the new is here!"
> — 2 Corinthians 5:17

"The kind of surrender that whispers—even if it costs something, I will follow You."

— FOUND

Chapter Eight
WHERE FAITH TOOK ROOT

As time passed, the transformation in me became more visible—even to my husband. I was all in with God. Every spare moment I had; I filled with Him.

I was reading Scripture, diving into devotionals, whispering prayers throughout the day.

But what I hadn't yet realised was just how much this shift was impacting the person who had been my other half for the past seventeen years.

Chris began to ask questions.

At first, they came gently—curious comments about how much time I was investing in church, in prayer, in Bible study. I brushed them off, assuming it was just a reaction to the long work hours, the home renovations, the busyness of life.

But deep down, I sensed something else. There was a quiet ache, a subtle grief over how much of me now belonged to Someone else.

We had always been inseparable. So I understood why this change felt confronting.

My life had taken on new meaning, new purpose, and with it, new rhythms.

Rhythms that didn't revolve around our old routine but around the presence of God. The man who once had all of me now felt like he had to share me with a God he couldn't see or understand.

And while I longed to walk closely with God, I never wanted to walk away from my husband. I didn't want my spiritual growth to become a wedge between us. I wanted to be deeply faithful to both.

One night, that tension reached the surface. We had a heartfelt conversation. I explained that my faith wasn't a phase. It was a lifelong commitment, a new way of living.

I reassured him of my love—that I wasn't leaving him behind, but I was also standing firm in my walk with God.

I told him gently, *"The evidence isn't just going to fall in your lap"* and then I gave him space.

That night, the over-thinker in me spiralled. I lay in bed, tears soaking the pillow. My heart felt torn in two—how could I ever choose between God and the man I loved? How could something that felt so right stir such tension in the relationship I held most dear?

I cried out to God, begging Him not to make me choose. My prayers came in whispers, soaked in fear and longing.

I told Him I still wanted to be that butterfly—that new creation He was shaping me into. I wanted to keep growing, but I didn't want to lose Chris in the process.

I turned the pages of my Bible, searching for something, anything, that would bring clarity.

And then I found it:

> "To the married I give this command (not I, but the Lord): A wife must not separate from her husband."
> — 1 Corinthians 7:10

Paul was addressing people like me—believers married to those who had not yet come to faith. And the message was clear: *stay. Hold on. Let God work.*

Marriage is still sacred, even when it stretches us. Even when we don't see eye to eye. It's holy ground when we let God stand in the middle.

So the next morning, before the sun rose and the kids stirred, I knelt beside my bed and gave it all to

God again. I wouldn't choose. I trusted Him with my marriage, with my husband, with our future. It was terrifying. But it was surrender.

The kind of surrender that whispers—even if it costs something, I will follow You.

That evening, I walked through the front door, still dreading another hard conversation. Chris was in the kitchen, making dinner, phone propped up beside him. I glanced at the screen, expecting the usual building projects or footy game—but instead, I froze.

He was watching a series called *Give Me an Answer* by Pastor Cliffe Knechtle.

I stared at the screen. Then back at him. Then back at the screen.

This was the same man who had just days earlier questioned everything. Now, he was watching a series that may just give him the answers.

Seeking. Curious. Open.

I didn't say much. I couldn't. My heart was silently praising God, the tears already forming.

> "For everyone who asks receives; the one who seeks finds; and to the one who knocks, the door will be opened." —Matthew 7:8

That night, we sat and continued to watch the series together. Cliffe answered tough questions with Scripture and grace, and we both felt drawn in.

It was a turning point. Not just for Chris. For us. Our hearts were being shaped—his through exploration, mine through answered prayers.

The evidence doesn't always fall in your lap—but God knows how to place it gently in your path.

My bold prayer had been heard. God wasn't just listening—*He was moving.*

"Now faith is confidence in what we hope for and assurance about what we do not see." — Hebrews 11:1

Soon after, Easter Camp approached. I packed nervously. It would be my first time attending the *WA Seventh-day Adventist Easter Camp*—and the first time I'd spent a night away from my family willingly in years.

The drive was full of butterflies. I was anxious. But I also felt God nudging me: *Step out. I'll meet you there.*

Emily had offered for me to stay in her caravan. Seeing her smiling face the moment I arrived settled my nerves. I spotted Brenna, Kim, Heather, and a few others, too.

Familiar faces in a sea of hundreds. It felt like God had scattered these friendships in my life ahead of time—little reminders that I wasn't walking into this alone.

The first worship service overwhelmed me. The music echoed through the marquee; voices lifted in praise. I didn't know many of the songs, but I sang them, through teary eyes.

Worship music became a new love language for me—a sacred space where my soul felt heard and held. I could feel the Holy Spirit in the room—soft, strong, present.

I tried new foods, including haystacks (which I originally thought were horse feed!). But a quick Google search cleared that up: vegetarian nachos.

Emily kindly began preparing them, but I had warned her—nothing spicy for me. After a past surgery, anything spicy caused serious indigestion, and I didn't want to be stuck at Easter camp with burning gastric pain.

She pulled out a red vegetable that looked like something between a capsicum and a chilli. We both tried a small piece to make sure it wasn't too spicy—it seemed mild enough, so she chopped it up.

She then handed me the knife to try Nutolene, another new food, and so I tasted it politely. Within seconds my mouth begun to burn.

I smiled through it, trying not to panic, thinking: *why didn't she warn me?*

We eventually worked out what had happened. Turns out, it wasn't the Nutolene—it was Chilli residue on the knife!

It didn't take long to figure it out. The culprit wasn't the Nutolene, it was chili residue on the knife! Moments later Emily took a bite of the red vegetable we had thought was a capsicum and instantly reached for the milk.

We both burst out laughing, picking out the fiery red pieces from our bowls and joking about it for the rest of our short but sweet time together. It was one of my highlights.

It was simple, funny, and oddly holy. Because in those laughs, I felt at home. Not just with Emily, or the people—but with myself. With whom I was becoming.

Camp wasn't just about the messages and music—it was also filled with quiet, meaningful moments of connection and joy.

I spent time with Brenna, Heather, Kim, and a few other warm, welcoming faces. We played games I'd never even heard of—most of which I lost—but it wasn't about winning. It was about laughing together, sharing stories, and just being present.

Even though I was only there for a day or two, something about it felt sacred. There was a sense of belonging that ran deeper than surface-level friendship.

It felt like stepping into a glimpse of what true community was meant to be—like family, knit together by something bigger than us.

I left camp changed. Not in a loud or dramatic way—but stronger, steadier, and more certain that my faith was beginning to take root in good soil.

Something had settled in me, something real. I knew I wanted to come back next year—and this time, I wanted to bring my whole family with me.

When they pulled up beside the garden gates to pick me up, their smiles felt like sunlight after a long winter.

I climbed into the car with more than just a bag of clothes and memories. I was carrying something sacred—something I couldn't quite explain, but I knew I was meant to share it with them.

"And let us consider how we may spur one another on toward love and good deeds, not giving up meeting together, as some are in the habit of doing, but encouraging one another—and all the more as you see the Day approaching." — Hebrews 10:24-25

Chapter Nine
STEPPING OUT IN FAITH

The next day was Sabbath, and I was back home—still buzzing after Easter Camp.

My heart was full, my mind racing, and my soul stirred. The things I had learnt, the stories I had heard, the people I had connected with—it all lingered, like the final notes of a worship song that still echoed in my spirit.

I was excited for Sabbath. Not just because it offered physical rest, but because it was becoming a sacred space for me.

A time to reflect, to be still, to journal, and to go deeper in my relationship with Jesus.

> *"Remember the Sabbath by keeping it holy."*
> *— Exodus 20:8*

Over the past few months, I have been learning more about the biblical Sabbath and what it truly meant to set aside the seventh day—Saturday—as a time of rest and renewal with God.

At first, it felt unfamiliar, even countercultural in a world that thrives on hustle and hurry.

But as I began to honour it, I noticed something shift inside me. The pause wasn't just good—*it was sacred.* It realigned me. It reminded me that I wasn't made to carry the weight of the world.

I was made to walk with God.

Chris, on the other hand—my husband—didn't exactly share my enthusiasm. He doesn't know how to stop moving. Whether it's the house renovations, weekend projects, or just his need to be productive, rest doesn't come naturally to him.

So, when he mentioned watching *The Bible Stories* miniseries he had found on YouTube while I was away, I nearly fell off my chair.

He asked if I wanted to watch it with him—ten full episodes, from Creation leading up to the Crucifixion and Resurrection of Jesus Christ.

This man, who could barely sit still for a movie, was now voluntarily pressing pause on his weekend to explore the Bible with me?

I didn't even hesitate. I curled up beside him on the couch and pressed play.

What followed were hours of shared moments—some confronting, others heartwarming, all of them meaningful.

We watched creation unfold, the fall of man, the flood, the exodus, the rise and fall of kings, the birth of Jesus, His ministry, death, and resurrection.

It was overwhelming and rich, and for someone still seeking—like Chris—it stirred up a lot of questions, for both of us.

I was scribbling notes the whole way through. But one moment hit both of us like a punch to the heart: *the massacre of the innocents.*

"When Herod realised he had been outwitted by the Magi, he was furious, and he gave orders to kill all the boys in Bethlehem and its vicinity who were two years old and under..." — Matthew 2:16

As a mother, that passage wrecked me. My heart shattered thinking about the grief of those parents.

How could a good and loving God allow something so horrendous? Why not strike down Herod instead?

I didn't have an answer. But I didn't turn away from God in that moment either. I wrestled. I cried. And I kept holding onto faith.

Because when we go back to Scripture, Jesus never promised a pain-free life.

In fact, He warned us:

> *"I have told you these things, so that in me you may have peace. In this world you will have trouble. But take heart! I have overcome the world."*
> *— John 16:33*

God never intended pain to be part of the story. His original design was one of harmony, joy, and peace.

But it was sin, introduced through human choice—that brought brokenness. And yet, even in our rebellion, God never turned His back on us.

He stepped into the brokenness Himself.

That's what gives me hope. Because though He may not always stop the storm, He never leaves us in it alone.

He walks with us through it.

He carries us when we're too weak to stand.

He surrounds us with peace when everything else is crumbling.

And when the answers don't come, He holds us through the questions.

Even more—*He redeems what's broken.*

He takes the ashes and makes something beautiful.

Sometimes it's the very thing we begged Him to take away that becomes the soil where our deepest trust in Him grows.

Another question that stuck with me from our viewing was this: *Why didn't Jesus stay longer on earth after His resurrection?*

He had just risen from the dead—why not spend more time proving it to more people?

I brought this up during our next *"question time"* with my boss and his wife. Their home had become a welcoming place for exploring faith, and their patience and wisdom often met my questions with grace and clarity.

They explained that Jesus had a specific purpose in those forty days after His resurrection: to prepare His disciples for the mission ahead.

If He had stayed longer, people might have depended solely on His physical presence instead of learning to rely on the Holy Spirit.

It made sense. Brenna's words also hit home: If Jesus hadn't left, the movement might have stayed small. But in leaving, He empowered it to grow beyond what any of them could imagine.

Still, I wrestled. Wouldn't more people have believed if they could've seen Him with their own eyes?

But then I remembered His final words on the cross:

"It is finished." — John 19:30

He came to accomplish something specific—*something eternal.*

Jesus wasn't just a good teacher, a healer, or a moral guide. He came with a mission rooted in divine love and eternal purpose.

He came to reveal the Father—to show us what God is truly like in character, mercy, and heart.

The cross wasn't a tragic end; it was the victorious fulfilment of love's greatest act. He took our place, satisfying justice so mercy could flow freely.

Then, He rose again—defeating death, proving His power, and making a way.

And He offers eternal life—in heaven. A restored relationship with God.

His mission wasn't left incomplete.

Every promise, every prophecy, every purpose—fulfilled in full. Nothing was left undone.

"It is finished" wasn't a whisper of defeat—it was the triumphant cry of completion.

The forty days were a time of commissioning.

"Then he opened their minds so they could understand the Scriptures." — Luke 24:45

And so, the mission was complete, and He said it Himself:

"But very truly I tell you, it is for your good that I am going away. Unless I go away, the Advocate will not come to you..." — John 16:7

His ascension wasn't a departure—it was a handoff. His Spirit would now dwell in every believer. No longer was God's presence confined to one place or person.

"But you will receive power when the Holy Spirit comes on you; and you will be my witnesses... to the ends of the earth." — Acts 1:8

Jesus left so that the Church—us—could begin. *And that changed everything.*

The number forty in Scripture often marks a time of preparation or transformation.

Noah faced forty days of rain as the earth was renewed. Moses met with God on Mount Sinai for forty days, returning changed. The Israelites spent forty years in the wilderness learning to trust. Jonah gave Nineveh forty days to repent—and they did.

Jesus fasted forty days in the desert before beginning His ministry, and after His resurrection, He spent forty more teaching and preparing His disciples.

These *"forty"* moments aren't just about time—they're sacred spaces where God works deeply.

If you find yourself in your own *"forty"*, trust He's doing something holy in you too.

That afternoon, we also talked about something I had barely scratched the surface of before, something I wasn't exactly keen on discussing—Satan.

I had always thought of him as more of a symbolic villain than an actual being. But Scripture was clear. Lucifer had once been a radiant angel, cast down because of pride. He chose rebellion, and in doing so, led others astray—starting with Adam and Eve.

> *"The great dragon was hurled down—that ancient serpent called the devil, or Satan, who leads the whole world astray." — Revelation 12:9*

Another question rose again: Why put the tree in the Garden if God knew what would happen?

And again, the answer came back to *love*. Real love isn't coerced—it's chosen. God didn't create robots. He created us with free will, because He wanted relationship, not obligation. Without choice, there can be no true love.

By the end of our time together, my heart was heavy but full. There was so much to think about, so many truths to hold onto.

Chris still had doubts, and I understood that. But he was asking questions. He was seeking. And to me, that meant God was already at work in his heart.

We all joined in prayer that day—my boss, his wife, Chris, and I. We asked God to continue showing Himself to Chris in real and personal ways.

And I believed He would.

Prayer had already changed so much in my life. It had carried me through storms, opened doors I didn't even know existed, and drawn me closer to a God I never imagined could feel so near.

So I held tight to hope—hope that Chris's journey was unfolding in God's perfect timing. Hope that the seeds being planted would one day bloom.

And until then, I would keep praying.

And trusting.

Because I know now—*God knows exactly what He's doing.*

"Putting on the armour of God doesn't mean the battle is over—it means you're ready for it."

— FOUND

Chapter Ten
WHEN PRAYERS TURN PERSONAL

One evening, I received a phone call from my sister Casey—my best friend and confidante, who lives back home on the other side of the country. We talk as often as we can. She's always been the one I turn to when life feels too heavy.

When I started this journey with God, Casey was sceptical. I had assumed she was an atheist, but she later revealed she was agnostic—much like I had been before coming to know God. As a result, our conversations rarely touched on anything spiritual.

But this call would change that.

She started telling me about an unusual encounter. After clocking off from her shift as a train guard, she was walking down the stairs at the station when she noticed people handing out flyers. Normally, like me, she would avoid them entirely. But this time, something prompted her to take one. She glanced at the flyer.

The words *"Jesus loves you"* were printed on the front.

Just then, her phone rang. It was her ex-husband. Struggling to speak, he told her, "*Nakita has hung herself... but she's alive. Get to the hospital.*"

Casey dropped to the ground in a state of panic and disbelief. Nakita, her youngest daughter—only nineteen years old—had fought a long, heartbreaking battle with depression. She's my niece, my family, has the biggest smile, the sharpest wit, and a heart that has been through far too much.

The call Casey had feared every day had finally come—*but with a twist of mercy.*

Casey made it to the hospital just as Nakita began to regain consciousness. Miraculously, there were no major complications.

As she sat beside her daughter, she pulled the flyer out of her bag again and said to me on the phone, "*Maybe Jesus is real... Could this be a sign?*"

I was stunned.

Amid such trauma, she had begun to consider the possibility of God.

We stayed on the phone for hours. I shared everything about my journey with God—how He carried me through my own storm and continues to transform my life.

Then Casey asked me to pray with her. I had never prayed out loud with someone before, let alone with my sister. But I felt the Holy Spirit guiding me. I told her I'd pray first, and when I finished, I would leave space for her to join in if she felt she wanted to say something.

To my amazement—she did. And followed it with a simple, soft *"Amen."*

That night, I went to bed with a full heart.

I thanked God—not only for sparing Nakita's life, but for stirring something in Casey's heart.

That prayer marked the beginning of her journey with God.

I felt grateful that God gave me the boldness to speak up and the words to say. I could feel the Spirit move through that moment.

> *"In the same way, the Spirit helps us in our weakness. We do not know what we ought to pray for, but the Spirit himself intercedes for us through wordless groans." — Romans 8:26*

From that night on, I began to reflect more deeply on my purpose here on earth.

I came to believe that we are not random or meaningless beings. We were created by a *God of love* — for relationship, for purpose, and to reflect His light.

I desperately wanted to know what my unique purpose was.

But I eventually realised: even if I never find a specific title or role to define it, my mission is simply this — to live a godly life, to share Jesus with others, and to love like He loves.

That's our calling as believers: *to magnify Christ with our lives so that others might come to know Him too.*

> *"How, then, can they call on the one they have not believed in? And how can they believe in the one of whom they have not heard? And how can they hear without someone preaching to them?"*
> *— Romans 10:14*

That realisation led me here — to write this very book.

I started looking back through my journal, reading through the raw and honest reflections I'd penned during the early days of my faith.

Page after page told of my transformation.

And I thought—if my journey can encourage even one person to take a step toward God, then I have to share it. Vulnerability and all.

This was my loophole—the way I could reach people without ever preaching at them.

Everyone's journey is different. There's no perfect formula for how God works in us. But He is always working. And He's carved out a unique path for each of us.

We just need to be willing to walk it.

"Come and hear, all you who fear God; let me tell you what he has done for me." — Psalm 66:16

Back at Easter Camp, one of the speakers, Pastor Pavel Goia, had given a powerful message on prayer. I didn't get to hear him live, but I later watched his sermons online and was deeply moved.

He spoke about the power of believing that God will answer your prayers—not just hoping or guessing but truly believing.

That doesn't mean God always answers the way we expect. But we can be sure that He always answers according to His perfect plan.

To pray like that, we must first be willing to surrender all.

That word—*surrender*—has stayed with me. It reminded me of a worship song, *"I Surrender"* by All Sons & Daughters. It became an anthem during the darkest days of my husband's cancer scare.

The message was simple yet soul-stirring: lay it all down, let go of my own strength, and trust that everything I needed was found in God alone.

I would sit in the stillness, letting that truth sink in as the music played.

It was more than a song—it was my prayer.

Pavel reminded us that to truly surrender, we must understand the cross. Jesus willingly went to Calvary to die in our place. He sacrificed Himself for us. Think about that.

Would you give your life for the entire world?

His love is beyond comprehension.

> *"Whoever does not take up their cross and follow me is not worthy of me."* — Matthew 10:38

Jesus calls us to take up our own crosses—to live surrendered lives, and then to go out and make disciples.

But before He gave that instruction, Jesus asked His disciples to wait and pray.

Why? Because prayer is our connection to the power source.

> *"Remain in me, as I also remain in you. No branch can bear fruit by itself; it must remain in the vine. Neither can you bear fruit unless you remain in me." — John 15:4*

I started to realise that the more I sought God—the more I *"plugged in"*—the more Satan began to show up in my life.

It was terrifying.

There were moments when I wanted to pull back from God because I felt too weak to fight off the attacks.

But I was reminded: *I don't fight alone.*

> *"Finally, be strong in the Lord and in his mighty power. Put on the full armour of God, so that you can take your stand against the devil's schemes."*
> *— Ephesians 6:10-11*

When I read those verses in Ephesians about the full armour of God, I began to picture it—really picture it.

I imagined myself standing tall, clothed head to toe in the armour He provides. And as each flaming arrow from the evil one came hurling toward me, it didn't destroy me.

Instead, it ricocheted off my shield of faith—each time bouncing back and striking the enemy. Not because of anything I had done, but because I kept choosing, again and again, to turn back to God.

I told myself that as long as I stood firm—rooted in His truth, His righteousness, His peace, His salvation, and His Word—the enemy would eventually grow tired. That maybe the attacks would slow down. But even if they didn't, I knew one thing for sure: *God's armour would never fail me.*

That moment of discouragement I'd felt—it gave way to a renewed strength. I was reminded that even in our weakness, God is strong.

When the path narrows, God is still the one leading us through.

It's never really about our own plan. It's always been about surrendering to His. We can do nothing apart from Him.

Wearing the armour didn't mean the battle was over—it meant I was ready for it.

The attacks didn't stop, but as long as I kept turning to God, I no longer felt defeated. I no longer questioned if I should retreat. I was equipped to move forward, one faithful step at a time.

Another truth that struck me came from Pastor Pavel Goia's teaching on the power of prayer.

He pointed out something that stayed with me: in the Bible, there are countless examples of people praying together—intentionally, persistently, with one heart and mind.

It made me realise that although we pray together in church each Sabbath, it's often not the kind of intentional, unified prayer he was talking about.

Putting on the armour of God is powerful.

But prayer?

Prayer is a weapon, too.

Jesus said that when two or three gather in His name, He is right there with them. That's not a metaphor. That's a promise.

"Again, truly I tell you that if two of you on earth agree about anything they ask for, it will be done for them by my Father in heaven. For where two or three gather in

> *my name, there am I with them."*
> *— Matthew 18:19-20*

Imagine the power of people gathering in prayer—not just casually, but intentionally—agreeing on what to pray for and lifting it up again and again... until.

That was something I loved about how Pastor Pavel would phrase it. He wouldn't put a time limit on prayer.

He would simply say, *"Pray... until."*

Because there's no formula for how long we should pray for something. There's no set number of days or years. We just keep praying until the answer comes.

And when nothing seems to happen—when weeks turn into months, and months stretch into years—we can easily wonder if God is even listening. But it's in those times we must remember: the delay is not denial.

The waiting is not wasted. God is working in a big way, unfolding a plan far greater than we can see.

There's something powerful that happens when people unite in prayer. It brings blessings. It stirs humility, grows unity, and multiplies love.

The Bible is filled with stories of prayers answered—some almost immediately, others only after long seasons of silence and perseverance.

Joseph waited thirteen years for his dream to unfold. Abraham waited twenty-five years for his promised son. Noah waited 120 years before the first drop of rain.

But they didn't give up. They kept trusting. They kept believing.

And they kept praying—until.

> *"I wait for the LORD, my whole being waits, and in his word I put my hope." — Psalm 130:5*

Throughout my journey, the challenges have been many. But so have the blessings.

Every battle has brought growth.

Every prayer has brought me closer to the heart of God.

And though Satan tries to steal, kill, and destroy—I now know where to turn.

I choose to stay plugged in.

Because I know now... *I was never meant to do this on my own.*

Chapter Eleven
Touching His Cloak

After the birth of our third child, I began to struggle with my health in a way I hadn't anticipated.

The pain became a regular companion—*relentless, unpredictable, and exhausting.*

One day, as I was searching for comfort, I came across the story of the woman who had been bleeding for twelve long years.

It's told in the gospels of Matthew, Mark, and Luke.

She had tried everything. No doctor could help. No treatment worked.

But then, in desperation and faith, she reached for Jesus. She didn't ask for a word, a touch, or even His attention.

> *"If I can just touch His cloak, I will be healed."*
> *— Mark 5:28*

Driven by faith, she touched Him—and she was healed.

> *"He said to her, 'Daughter, your faith has healed you. Go in peace and be freed from your suffering.'"*
> — Mark 5:34

That story moved me deeply because it resonated with my own suffering.

For nine long years, I endured countless tests, procedures, emergency room visits, hospital admissions, and long, painful days confined to bed.

My body would flare with agony once a month, sometimes for weeks at a time. And as time went on, it only got worse.

Every treatment that once gave hope eventually stopped working. I had no answers—only more questions and dead ends. Pain became something I had to live with.

I advocated fiercely for myself. I believed healing might come, but my voice often felt lost in a sea of dismissals.

Women's health—well, that's a whole story of its own. I won't unpack that here. But let's just say, I was tired—physically, emotionally, and spiritually.

Still, I kept telling myself, *"Where there is struggle, there is hope".* I held onto the belief that maybe the next flare would be the last.

That maybe healing was just around the corner.

One night, the pain hit harder than ever before. It was unbearable. My body was restless, my mind clouded, and no position brought relief.

I ended up in our local hospital, again, desperate for anything to ease the intensity. By morning, I was being sent for yet another scan—this one in the city, a two-hour drive away.

As I reached the car that morning, still dazed and exhausted, the rain started to sprinkle as we walked slowly to the car, and something unexpected happened.

We were flagged down.

It was my boss and several others. They had come—not with medical advice or questions—but with prayer. Right there, in the drizzling rain, in the hospital car park, they surrounded me and prayed.

It's a moment I'll never forget.

I was weary, broken, and in immense pain. But their voices rose in unity and love, and in that moment, the Holy Spirit moved through them.

I call it the *Carpark Prayer*.

That prayer didn't erase my pain, but it filled me with something greater — *gratitude*.

Gratitude for a God who strengthens us in our weakness. Gratitude for people who let the Spirit lead. And gratitude for the reminder that I wasn't fighting alone.

Before knowing God, I would let my pain consume me. I was angry. Frustrated. Hopeless. I battled alone.

The dismissals, the unanswered questions, the treatments that failed — it all felt like the world was against me.

But as I got to know Jesus, something shifted. I still hurt, but I no longer felt hopeless. I began to believe that maybe my suffering served a purpose only God understood.

> *"Heal me, Lord, and I will be healed; save me and I will be saved, for you are the one I praise."*
> *— Jeremiah 17:14*

Recently, I chose a Bible study plan titled *"Healed by Jesus"* to complete in our Bible Buddies' group. I chose it out of desperation—I needed reassurance, a reminder that Jesus still heals.

I've never been the type to wallow in self-pity, but I'd be lying if I said the repeated knockdowns weren't wearing me down.

It was especially hard when the pain began to affect my family, my work, and my ability to show up in the ways I wanted to.

Sometimes the weight of it all felt unbearable.

In my attempts to stay grounded, I would often compare my suffering to others who had it worse. It helped me keep perspective, reminded me to not stay down for too long, to rise back up, and to be strong.

But deep down, one lesson that stood out to me was this:

We all need healing in one way or another.

Whether it's physical, emotional, mental, or spiritual—Jesus came for all of it.

During the study, I found myself reflecting on how people flocked to Jesus when He walked the earth.

Jesus healed people with compassion, power, and purpose. He didn't turn away the sick, the outcast, or the desperate—instead, He moved toward them.

The blind received sight, the lame walked, the deaf heard, and the lepers were cleansed.

He spoke healing with just a word, touched the untouchable, and restored not only bodies but hearts and lives.

Each miracle revealed His divine authority and deep love.

No illness was too great, no person too far gone.

Whether in crowded streets or quiet corners, Jesus met people in their pain and left them changed. And though I am sure there were many stories not recorded, we know that countless lives were transformed simply by being in His presence.

He is still that same miracle worker today.

The challenge for us now is to trust that He is working, even when we don't see it right away.

To have eyes that are open to His movement.

To not become stagnant in our waiting, but to wait with anticipation.

I'm learning to trust that Jesus is doing something in me and through me, even in the waiting. Especially in the waiting.

And I pray we all learn to trust in God's perfect timing.

One story I love is from John 9—about the man born blind. The disciples asked Jesus whether the man's blindness was due to his sin or his parents. It was a common belief at that time. But Jesus gave an answer that shifted everything.

> *"Neither this man nor his parents sinned," said Jesus, "but this happened so that the works of God might be displayed in him." — John 9:3*

What a powerful truth.

Sometimes our suffering is not punishment.

Its purpose.

That we may become the vessel through which God displays His power.

In this case, Jesus chose a strange method. He spat on the ground, made mud with His saliva, and smeared it on the man's eyes. Then He told him to go wash in the pool of Siloam.

When the man did, his sight was restored.

Jesus could have simply spoken healing, as He did for others. But He didn't. Why?

I don't know.

But I do know this — He meets each of us uniquely.

His healing comes in different forms, different timings, and in different ways. We just have to trust that His plan is always good.

This story also challenged my perspective.

What if, instead of focusing on the healing I haven't received, I thanked God for the suffering He has spared me from?

What if I stopped asking, *"Why me?"* and started asking, *"What now, Lord?"*

If I am meant to be healed, I believe I will be.

But that decision belongs to God, not me.

In the meantime, I will choose to live for Jesus — *even from the middle of the storm.*

Miracles surround us.

While I wait for mine, I will celebrate others.

I'll rejoice in their healing, their breakthrough, their answered prayer—because their miracle is proof that God is still moving.

I'll choose to look for the small, quiet wonders of His presence.

The kind we so often overlook.

A moment of laughter after a flood of tears.
A stillness in the chaos.
A peace that comes when it shouldn't.

These are miracles, too.

Evidence that He is near, that He sees us, and that His grace is still enough—even here, even now.

Let us have eyes to see.
Let us not be stagnant in our waiting.
Let us trust in the God who heals.

He is always working—in us, around us, and through us.

Chapter Twelve
GRACE FOR THE HARD DAYS

One morning, as I packed the kids into our trusty old 4WD—the same one that carried us around Australia for several years—I pulled out of the driveway and instantly sensed something was wrong.

I couldn't explain it, just that it felt... off.

I rang my husband as I crawled down the street. He was out of town but promised he'd check it when he got back. In the meantime, I cautiously made the school drop-offs, silently praying for our safety with each kilometre. Not that there were many living in a small country town.

When I pulled into work, just a metre shy of my usual parking spot, there was a horrible screech, and the car suddenly dropped. I quickly shut off the engine and got out to inspect.

The front wheel arch arm had snapped clean in half—it looked like one corner of the car had face-planted into the gravel.

My first reaction was not panic. It was praise. *Praise God!*

I got the kids to school safely. I made it to work.

This couldn't have been better timing as I realised that break could've happened on the highway, with my children in the back. But it didn't. God's protection was over us.

Once the shock had settled, I felt a strange mix of emotions. Sadness that this might be the end of the old girl, our faithful road-tripping companion.

And then a tiny flicker of excitement—maybe a new car was in my future?

But, just like my husband helped repair me all those years ago, he fixed her up too—fit as a fiddle a short week later.

While the car was being repaired, I was stuck without transport. Before I even had time to consider how I'd manage school runs and work, my boss generously offered to loan me his wife's car.

I was overwhelmed with gratitude, but hesitant to accept—how could she go without a car for my sake?

Before I could even finish saying no, she showed up at my workplace and handed me the keys.

I couldn't believe it.

These selfless, godly people—how grateful I was that God had placed them in my life.

Their generosity, their willingness to go without so I wouldn't have to... I was humbled.

Driving her fancy car that started with the push of a button (and which I drove like a nervous old lady), I couldn't stop thinking about how God shows up in both big and small ways.

> *"A generous person will prosper; whoever refreshes others will be refreshed"* — Proverbs 11:25

That day reminded me of something profound: being a Christian isn't just a title we wear—it's a life we live.

It's reflected in the choices we make when no one is watching, in the sacrifices we're willing to make for others, and in the kindness we extend without expecting anything in return.

As I held those borrowed car keys in my hand, I realised this was more than an act of generosity—*it was a living example of Christlike love.*

These people didn't help me because it was convenient; they helped because their hearts beat in rhythm with His.

The world often measures worth by what we keep, but God measures it by what we give. And my boss and his wife gave freely—just as Jesus gave His life for us.

In that moment, I felt the heartbeat of the gospel: *love in action.*

> *"Do nothing out of selfish ambition or vain conceit. Rather, in humility value others above yourselves."*
> *— Philippians 2:3*

When Paul wrote *Philippians 2:3,* he was describing exactly what I had witnessed. Their humility, their willingness to go without so I wouldn't have to—*that's what it means to follow Jesus.*

Driving that borrowed car, I couldn't stop thinking: *This is Christianity.*

Not just words spoken on Sabbath, but faith expressed through selflessness, generosity, and grace.

They didn't just tell me about God's love—they showed me. And in doing so, they reminded me that when we choose to serve others, we reflect Jesus to a watching world.

> *"In the same way, let your light shine before others, that they may see your good deeds and glorify your Father in heaven." — Matthew 5:16*

June rolled around before I could even blink, bringing with it another wave of challenges—but I was more spiritually equipped than ever before.

I had learnt to fully trust God with everything life threw at me. Mostly.

As mothers, we carry this innate pull to protect our children, to keep them safe and emotionally secure.

Our eldest daughter Chloe had been struggling with her mental health for some time, and though we were navigating it together, mainstream high school life was proving increasingly difficult for her.

Teenage pressures, toxic peer relationships, and a world that often demands perfection took their toll.

Thankfully, we've always had a strong bond and open communication. And one day she opened up to me about what was weighing her down.

What she shared lit a fire in me. I was angry. I was heartbroken. I wanted to fix it—now.

But being part of a small town and school community, and working in a public role, I had to calm myself before acting.

I couldn't let my emotions lead—I had to let God.

My first response was to ask my church family to pray for her.

That decision became the key that unlocked a door in her heart—a door to faith.

I told her the church was praying for her, and we started talking deeply about who God is, how He works, and the blessings that had already poured over our family.

I reminded her that she's never truly alone. God is with her, even in this.

She wasn't ready for therapy or medication, but she was willing to try something else—so I suggested she find a quiet place on our five-acre property, sit still, and just talk to God.

Pour it all out. He's listening, I told her. *He will give you strength.*

Being a teenager in today's society—and having not grown up with a foundation of faith—comes with its own unique set of challenges when it comes to building a relationship with God.

The pressures of fitting in, the constant pull of social media, and the overwhelming noise of cultural opinions often drown out the still, small voice of truth.

There is a growing stigma around Christianity in this generation—a perception that faith is outdated, restrictive, or irrelevant.

I knew from the beginning that her journey toward God wouldn't be simple or straightforward. It couldn't be something I forced or controlled for her or any of my children.

As much as I longed for them to know the peace, strength and purpose that came from walking with Jesus, I realised I had to surrender that longing fully to Him.

Her path would need to be her own.

So, I did the only thing I truly could—I placed her journey into God's hands, trusting that He loves her even more than I do and in His perfect timing, He would work on her heart.

Later that day, and to my surprise, she let me download the Bible app on her phone, and together—with a little convincing—we started a devotional titled *"A Teen's Guide to: Knowing Who God Is"*. It became a sacred connection point for us both—a seed planted.

I just had to leave it up to God to keep watering it.

One Scripture verse, in particular, stuck with me—and I prayed it would cling to her heart like glue:

"The Lord your God is with you, the Mighty Warrior who saves. He will take great delight in you; in his love he will no longer rebuke you, but will rejoice over you with singing." — Zephaniah 3:17

What a powerful truth: *God is for us.* He rejoices over us. He is our comforter and defender.

And yet, as a mother, it's hard not to be consumed with anger toward those who hurt your child.

But even in that, I was challenged: *What would Jesus do?* I thought.

The answer, I already knew: He would pray for them.

"Bless those who curse you, pray for those who mistreat you." — Luke 6:28

This command from Jesus shook me.

Could I really pray for those who hurt my daughter?

It took time, but eventually—I did.

When I finally stopped stewing in my frustration and started praying for the people who had caused the hurt, something inside me shifted.

I felt a strange sense of renewal. A release.

Instead of taking my anger out on them or venting to someone else, I learnt to bring it to God. To talk to Him about it. And somehow, that made all the difference.

It didn't happen overnight. It took a long time before I could sincerely pray for the ones who had mistreated my daughter.

But now, when someone grinds my gears, my first response is prayer. No hesitation.

And the sooner I pray, the calmer I feel.

There's power in obedience — even when it's hard.

Learning to pray for those who hurt me or the ones I love stirred a bigger question in my heart:

What does it really mean to behave like a Christian?

I began to reflect on my own life — not in a box-checking, performance-based way, but with the deep desire to reflect Jesus in everything I did.

As my boss once wisely said, *"Jesus gets all the ticks."* He is the only perfect one.

And He also gave us the perfect example to follow.

Over the past year, I'd been growing in my relationship with Him—reading the Gospels, learning about His public ministry, and discovering what it meant to live a godly life.

I was reading my Bible every day, and often I'd go over the same verses repeatedly, needing the words to sink in—especially on days when distractions made it hard to focus.

What I've come to learn is this:

The Bible isn't a book you read once and put back on the shelf. It's a lifelong journey. A well of wisdom that never runs dry.

I'd sit in church and hear others reference Scripture, effortlessly recalling where it came from, and I remember thinking, *I want to know it like that.*

Not just the words—but where they came from and what they really mean.

I had my favourites—verses I clung to and recited often.

But the first one I ever truly memorised, and one that still speaks to the deepest part of me, is from the book of Philippians:

"I can do all this through him who gives me strength."
— Philippians 4:13

It reminds me that I am not weak, not with Christ.

He strengthens me.

Through every hardship, through every challenge, I have access to His power.

I prayed consistently—morning before the kids woke, evening after dinner, and often throughout the day.

My prayer life became the lifeline that kept me connected to God.

I brought Him everything—my praise, my struggles, my confessions, my requests.

I learnt to rely more on the Holy Spirit.

I tried so hard to let go of perfectionism, I stopped working to impress others and instead worked to please God.

Church became my refuge. I rarely missed a Sabbath service. Even when I was physically unwell, I still went.

And every time, *He carried me through.*

Chapter Thirteen
TO LOVE AND LET GO

Everything I've experienced on this journey has taught me one powerful truth: *let love be the ruling principle in my life.*

I still remember the moment I fell in love with my husband. We had only been together a few months when we discovered I was pregnant.

Fear gripped me—not just about becoming a mother so young, but the terrifying possibility of doing it alone. I had seen too many stories like mine where the fathers fled at the news. And to be honest, I didn't have much trust in men at that point in my life.

But then Chris said something I'll never forget—*he was all in.*

He was over the moon to start a family with me, even with our poor circumstances. In that moment, fear gave way to trust, and trust grew into love. It was instant. Deep. Real.

I didn't think I could ever experience a greater love than the love I had for my husband and, later, for each of my children. But I was wrong.

When I chose God and truly got to know Him, I encountered a different kind of *love*.

At first, I thought the difference was that I now felt the love of God. But I came to realise—it wasn't just about being loved by Him. It was about loving Him back.

What is love like—real love—when you know that God loves you, and you love Him back?

It almost feels impossible to put into words. It's not like any earthly love. It's deeper, steadier, purer.

It's the kind of love that meets you in the darkest places and still calls you beloved. It's the love that saw every mistake you've ever made and chose you anyway. It's knowing that even when you mess up, God doesn't withdraw—*He draws nearer.*

He doesn't shame you; He restores you.

To be loved by God is to be known fully and still completely accepted. It's the quiet comfort of knowing you're never alone. It's peace that doesn't depend on your circumstances, and hope that doesn't run dry when things fall apart.

His love is relentless—chasing you down, lifting you up, and covering you with grace.

And to love Him back? *It changes everything.*

It shifts your priorities, your desires, your whole view of the world. It's no longer about earning love but responding to it.

Loving God means choosing Him again and again, even when it's hard.

It's wanting to be near Him—not because you have to, but because you can't imagine life without Him.

It's the most freeing love of all—one that gives more than it takes, one that satisfies every longing, one that doesn't fade or fail.

To be loved by God and to love Him back is to finally know what your soul was made for.

Jesus said it plainly:

"The most important one," answered Jesus, "is this: 'Hear, O Israel: The Lord our God, the Lord is one. Love the Lord your God with all your heart and with all your soul and with all your mind and with all your strength.' The second is this: 'Love your neighbour as yourself.' There is no commandment greater than these." — Mark 12:29-31

Loving God with all that I am — *the greatest commandment.*

It wasn't just a shift in belief; it was a shift in how I experienced the world.

As my love for God deepened, so did my love for my husband, my children, and even for people I hadn't yet met.

His love didn't just fill me — it overflowed from me.

Suddenly, I saw others not through my own limited lens, but through His eyes — eyes of compassion, grace, and understanding.

God's love transformed my perspective.

Ordinary moments became sacred.

The sky looked bluer, the breeze felt softer, the simplest things — like a laugh from my child, or the stillness of a quiet morning — felt rich with meaning.

It wasn't that life became perfect, but I had come to know the One who is, the One who created it all.

And knowing Him made all the difference.

His love awakened me to beauty I'd never noticed, to purpose I hadn't understood, and to a joy that couldn't be shaken — even on the hard days.

Loving God didn't just change my heart; it changed how I lived, how I loved, and how I saw the world.

"Dear friends, let us love one another, for love comes from God. Everyone who loves has been born of God and knows God. Whoever does not love does not know God, because God is love." — 1 John 4:7-8

One of the hardest personal battles I've faced is perfectionism—not the kind that pushes you to do better, but the kind that quietly steals your peace. The kind that whispers you're never enough.

For a long time, I felt like I was drowning beneath the pressure to be flawless, to meet an invisible standard that constantly moved just out of reach.

Eventually, I had to dig deep and ask myself: *Why do I carry this exhausting need to prove myself?*

What I uncovered was painful but necessary.

My perfectionism wasn't about excellence—it was about approval. Deep down, I believed that if I wasn't perfect, I wasn't worthy. That if I messed up, I was a failure. But God, in His mercy, began unravelling that lie.

He showed me that growth is found in the mess. That grace often greets us in the very places we try to hide. He reminded me that learning comes through stumbling, that mistakes are part of being human.

Slowly, I began to see perfectionism not as a strength to be admired, but as a mask—a weakness disguised as control. And I started letting go.

I'm learning—day by day—that it's okay to be imperfect. It's okay to fall short. Because I no longer live for the approval of others, I live to please the One who already loves me as I am.

I'm not chasing perfection anymore—*I'm following the One who is perfect.*

I still pray often for Jesus to help me with this, and He does. In small, sacred ways, He shows me what freedom looks like. Every day, I notice glimmers of release in the places I used to feel so bound.

I now see myself clearly: a sinner, made righteous through Christ alone, walking forward not in the pursuit of flawlessness, but in the pursuit of faithfulness.

When Kim learnt how passionate I was about music, she began sending me worship songs.

And it was literal music to my ears; music has played a healing role I didn't expect. The words of worship songs have a way of speaking directly to the parts of me still learning to rest in grace.

When I hear lyrics about God's love, His mercy, and my identity in Christ, something inside me softens.

The pressure loosens. My heart remembers who I am—not because of what I've done, but because of what Jesus has done for me.

Music has helped reshape my thoughts, pushing back against perfectionism with truth and lifting my eyes to the One who never asks me to earn His love.

I've always loved to sing—though only in the privacy of my home, usually with my family as my daily audience. Whether they appreciate it or not, they're treated to a full-blown morning concert as I step out of my room, playlist in hand and heart wide open.

That playlist continues to grow—thanks in large part to Kim, and Brenna, who has since joined in on this mission to find the most amazing worship songs.

One song that quickly became a favourite for both me and my daughter Emileigh was *"I'm So Blessed"* by CAIN.

Its message was pure joy—uplifting, honest, and full of life.

We loved it so much that we wanted to hear it at church. When I mentioned it to my boss and his wife, they didn't just smile politely—they invited us over to practice.

That night, Emileigh lit up as she led everyone in the actions she'd carefully choreographed for the song. My boss's wife graciously learnt to play it on the piano, just in time for that Sabbath. Watching my daughter glow with joy and confidence in that moment was unforgettable—pure delight radiated from her face.

And now, every time that song plays in church, I'm reminded not just of a catchy tune, but of a small miracle—a moment of joy that was born from release, from connection, from grace.

Perfection never gave me that kind of joy. But Jesus did. And still does.

"Come, let us sing for joy to the LORD; let us shout aloud to the Rock of our salvation. Let us come before him with thanksgiving and extol him with music and song."
— Psalm 95:1-2

Before I knew it, it was early July, a little over a year since that simple conversation led me to open the Bible for the first time.

That Sabbath, Mr. Hester was leading Bible study.

We were about to dive into Mark 14 when he paused to share a message.

I don't know if it was planned or if the Holy Spirit was leading, but he spoke about God's promise and the second coming of Jesus.

That one word—*soon*—hit me hard.

I couldn't stop thinking about it for weeks.

Jesus is coming soon.

But how soon?

And... am I ready?

More than that—is my family?

The thought of heaven without them brought me to tears.

If Jesus came tomorrow, would I ever see some of my loved ones again? The ones who were yet to accept Jesus into their life.

The anxiety crept in as I wrestled with what it means to die without accepting Christ. But I soon began to find peace in God's Word.

When we die, the Bible describes it as sleep—a peaceful, unconscious rest.

But when Jesus returns, those who have died in Him will rise first, followed by those still alive in Christ—and together, we will meet the Lord in the air.

Jesus has already paid for our sins, and those who are His have nothing to fear.

The judgment reveals that we are covered by His righteousness and are ready to be with Him forever.

> *"For the wages of sin is death, but the gift of God is eternal life in Christ Jesus our Lord."*
> *— Romans 6:23*

Those who did not accept Jesus will rise in the second resurrection, after the thousand years, to face the final judgment.

Because they rejected Christ's sacrifice, their sins remain unpaid—and the wages of sin is death.

The Bible says they will be cast into the lake of fire, where they will be quickly consumed like dry stubble.

This is the second death—a permanent and final end.

But even in this, when you think about it, God is just and merciful, bringing sin and suffering to a close forever.

"Surely they are like stubble; the fire will burn them up. They cannot even save themselves from the power of the flame. These are not coals for warmth; this is not a fire to sit by." — Isaiah 47:14

It's confronting.

And yet, it's merciful.

In one of our question times, my boss and his wife shared something that shifted my thinking.

They said heaven will be full of people who love and worship God.

For someone who never wanted anything to do with Him on earth, being surrounded by worship and praise would feel like torture.

Heaven wouldn't be heaven for them.

So, God, in His mercy, gives them an ending that's quick and just—not drawn-out suffering.

It's still hard to accept that some we love may not be with us in eternity, but I know God is loving and fair.

And He never stops reaching.

He continually offers opportunities for people to choose Him.

But ultimately, it's a choice.

God gives us that freedom—*even when it breaks His heart.*

Still, for us who believe, this isn't a gloomy subject—*it's one filled with hope.*

The first resurrection will usher us into the presence of God, into an eternal home where *love reigns.*

A place beyond anything we can imagine, where we'll thrive in God's presence, free from pain, sin, and sorrow. *Forever.*

"For my Father's will is that everyone who looks to the Son and believes in him shall have eternal life, and I will raise them up at the last day."
— John 6:40

What an incredible gift.

We were made to love God, love others, and live in the hope of eternity with Him.

And what an urgent reminder to share the gospel with those we love, and everyone else.

*"People may not always hear a sermon,
but they'll notice how you love."*

— FOUND

Chapter Fourteen
THE BOOKSTORE BREAKTHROUGH

August arrived, and with it came one of my favourite visitors—Pastor T. He made the long drive to preach every month or so, and I always looked forward to what message God would bring through him.

That Sabbath, he spoke on *compassion*—a message that struck me deeply.

He challenged us to examine our personal biases and to consider how Jesus responded when confronted by people who broke the law.

We turned to John 8—the story of the woman caught in adultery.

I'd heard it before, but that day, it felt like the words were being spoken straight to my heart.

The scene was intense—this woman, dragged out in front of a crowd by religious leaders, was likely terrified and humiliated.

The Pharisees, with their chests puffed up in false righteousness, weren't just accusing her—they were using her as bait to trap Jesus.

I pictured her, trembling, surrounded by men ready to stone her.

They asked Jesus what should be done. By law, she deserved death. But Jesus didn't take the bait.

Instead of condemning her or falling into their trap, Jesus offered a profoundly humbling response:

"When they kept on questioning him, he straightened up and said to them, 'Let any one of you who is without sin be the first to throw a stone at her.'" — John 8:7

That line pierced me.

How often had I held a stone in my own hand—maybe not physically, but in my heart?

Stone-throwing can come in so many forms:

Judgmental thoughts.
Unforgiveness.
Bitterness.

Jesus wasn't just talking to the Pharisees. *He was talking to all of us.*

One by one, the accusers dropped their stones and walked away, their silence louder than any argument.

And then, Jesus turned to the woman — not with anger, not with disdain, but with dignity.

"Jesus straightened up and asked her, 'Woman, where are they? Has no one condemned you?' 'No one, sir,' she said. 'Then neither do I condemn you,' Jesus declared. 'Go now and leave your life of sin.'"
— John 8:10-11

He didn't shame her.
He didn't excuse her sin either.
But He *met her with mercy* and pointed her toward a better way.

That moment redefined compassion for me.

Compassion isn't passive. It's not soft or weak.

It sees brokenness and speaks truth without abandoning love. It doesn't sweep sin under the rug, but it also doesn't weaponise it.

I sat in that church, quiet and undone.

How many times had I failed to extend that kind of compassion?

It was clear: if I wanted to follow Jesus, really follow Him, I needed to learn how to put my stones down.

To stop waiting until people were *"worthy"* of grace, and instead, start offering it freely, the way Jesus had with me.

That Sabbath, I didn't just hear about compassion—I experienced it.

In Scripture.
In conviction.
In the gentle voice of the Holy Spirit whispering: *this is how you are to love.*

And slowly, my heart began to change.

Later, over lunch, I sat down with Pastor T and shared about this very book.

I told him how writing this book had challenged me to be vulnerable, to lay bare all the rough patches of my journey.

I confessed how hard that was—but also how I hoped these words could become a key that unlocks the door for someone else to walk through and meet Jesus.

This book is the story of my walk, step by step, along a rocky, uneven path.

It's about the growth, the hard lessons, the miracles, and the moments of doubt.

And through it all, my steady—though often imperfect—*pursuit of Jesus.*

It's compassion that softens hearts, lifts shame, and creates space for grace to do its work.

And just like the woman Jesus met that day, I've learnt that it's compassion that often cracks open the door to transformation.

So if nothing else, may these pages remind someone—anyone—that Jesus still says:

"Neither do I condemn you"

And He still leads with love.

> *"Finally, all of you, be like-minded, be sympathetic, be compassionate and humble." — 1 Peter 3:8*

I wish I could say that from this point on, I never stumbled.

That once I surrendered fully to God, everything in life found its rhythm.

I wish I could say that my faith fixed every fracture and filled every gap in my heart and home.

But the truth is, faith doesn't erase our humanity. *It refines it.*

And somewhere along the way, as I was growing in my faith. I began to feel unbalanced.

At first, it was just a quiet undercurrent beneath the surface of my days. But it grew.

Between the demands of work, the weight of motherhood, and my deepening hunger to know God more, something else—someone else—began to slip from the centre of my attention.

I hadn't intended to neglect my role as a wife. I loved my husband deeply. But I was running out of emotional room.

The pace I was keeping, the spiritual fire within me, and the passion to grow in this new life with God—it all took up space I hadn't learnt how to share yet.

Part of what made it harder was walking this journey mostly alone within our home.

My husband, though kind and supportive, wasn't on the same path. He believed in God, but not in the way I had come to. Not with the same urgency. Not with the same surrender.

He wasn't resistant—he just wasn't ready.

Still, he respected what I believed. He often said he admired the peace it gave me. And I knew he meant it.

But that gentle difference between us became a quiet ache. It wasn't conflict. It was something deeper. A longing.

I wanted to share not just my life with him, but my faith—the deepest, most transformative part of who I was becoming.

He never once asked me to slow down or step away from God. He never stood in the way. But still, I could feel the distance growing—not because he was pulling away, but because I was.

I started to fill the empty spaces with church, with community, with service, and with study. All good things. All meaningful. But I had unknowingly started replacing the closeness we once shared with the comfort I found in other areas of my life.

I was chasing growth, but I wasn't inviting him into it. I was building a stronger faith, but I wasn't always building a stronger *us*.

And that wasn't fair to either of us.

Through prayer, time, and many humbling moments, I began to learn that unity in marriage doesn't mean we have to move at the same pace. It doesn't mean dragging someone forward or slowing ourselves down. It means making space for one another along the way.

It means holding hands, even when our strides are different.

Ellen G. White once wrote:

> "The strongest argument in favour of the gospel is a loving and lovable Christian." – The Ministry of Healing, p. 470

I come back to that often.

A loving and lovable Christian, to me, is someone who reflects Jesus not just in what they believe, but in how they live—how they treat people with kindness, patience, humility, grace, and genuine care.

It's not about being perfect; it's about being Christlike in the everyday, even in the mess.

I've come to realise that this kind of life becomes a powerful testimony because: *people may not always hear a sermon, but they'll notice how you love.*

I believe our lives speak louder than our words ever could.

And when our lives reflect His love, that's when others can truly begin to see the character of God in us.

So my job isn't to convince, to preach, or to push.

It's to *love*—consistently, patiently, without condition.

To let my life reflect the goodness of God so clearly that my husband can see the fruit of it, even if he hasn't yet tasted it himself.

So I hold onto hope. Not a pressured, anxious kind of hope—but a gentle, anchored one.

I believe in what's possible when love leads the way—not guilt, not fear, not obligation. *Just love.*

I believe that God is not only working in me, but in him too. Quietly. Tenderly. In ways I may never see or fully understand.

And as my husband continues to witness what God is doing in my life—the peace, the healing, the strength—I pray that something in him begins to stir.

Not because I need him to change.

Not even because I long for us to walk in perfect spiritual sync.

But because the same God who called *me* out of the dark... *is calling him, too.*

And I know—when the time is right—he'll hear Him.

The weekend was here, and we had time to spare in the big city before Emileigh's *One Big Voice* concert.

I'd never been to Koorong before—*a Christian bookstore*—despite hearing so many good things.

I decided this was the perfect opportunity to visit.

As we parked the car, Chris—still buckled in—looked over at me and said, *"Don't buy anything."*

I smiled.

Emileigh, grinning in the back seat, leaned forward and whispered, *"It's Mum. As if she's not going to buy something."*

For years, we'd lived paycheck to paycheck, barely scraping by.

And now, with a little more financial breathing room, I wrestled with the urge to make up for all the times we went without.

I knew I needed to reframe that mindset...but today wasn't that day.

Walking into Koorong felt like stepping into a wonderland. Shelves upon shelves of books. So many words. So much wisdom gathered in one place.

I had come for one specific title—a new release I'd seen online.

The moment I spotted the *"New Releases"* sign, I made a beeline for it.

As I ran my fingers along the spines, I imagined their truth and inspiration sinking into my soul with a single touch.

I found the book I was looking for and tucked it under my arm.

My plan was simple: check out book sizes, fonts, and page counts—anything that could help me with designing my own. But then another cover caught my eye. And another. And another.

Soon, my arms were full.

One book in particular stood out—*God's Big Picture: A Bible Overview* by Vaughan Roberts.

Just 130 pages. Clear, accessible.

It looked perfect for Chris.

Maybe this is it, I thought. Maybe this will provide him with what he is searching for.

It wasn't just a book—it was a gift. A small, thoughtful offering.

Not to push or persuade, but to gently show: *I see you. I care. And I want you to know the God who changed my life.*

After all, love speaks louder than words—and sometimes, what opens someone's heart to Jesus isn't a debate or a well-crafted argument, but a quiet invitation. A gentle nudge. A loving offering.

If this book holds the answer he's been searching for, maybe—just maybe—we can finally walk with God... together.

While I continued to browse, Emileigh discovered the children's section and excitedly led me to a book she wanted to buy with her pocket money.

She glanced at the growing pile in my arms and asked, "Mum... *you're not really going to buy all those books, are you?*"

I just smiled and nodded toward the counter.

I justified my pile with my upcoming birthday—and scored a 25% discount voucher for next time. (I decided right then that there would definitely be a next time.)

When the friendly woman at the counter asked if I wanted a bag, I smiled and said, *"Yes please".* What I didn't say was, *it's not really for carrying—it's to hide the evidence.*

I slipped my things inside and gave a polite smile.

Back in the car, Chris raised an eyebrow.

"I told you not to buy anything."

"But I bought you something!" I grinned, reaching for God's Big Picture.

"It's short. Just 130 pages. It even has diagrams!"

I was very pleased with myself.

That evening, I hinted at the book a few more times, not-so-subtly trying to spark his curiosity.

And then, after dinner, I walked into our bedroom and found him reading it.

My heart could have burst.

I wanted to lie next to him and just watch him read, but that would've been weird, so I grabbed one of my own new books and read too.

Soon, our youngest, Charlie, poked his head in.

"Is Dad reading a book?" he asked, confused.

Emileigh followed.

"Dad, you said you don't read!"

Even our eldest walked past, did a double-take, and said, "Is Dad reading?"

He was. Three chapters in.

When he finally closed it, I asked, "Did you learn anything?"

He grinned.

"Yes. The most important thing—God made man first. Then He made a woman to serve the man and be His companion."

He smirked cheekily.

I laughed and shook my head, but inside, my heart was glowing.

> "The LORD God said, "It is not good for the man to be alone. I will make a helper suitable for him."
> — Genesis 2:18

You can read further from this point in *Genesis* to find out how *"Woman"* was made from man.

It might've started with a cheeky comment, but something had shifted.

That book—*that gift*—was more than pages and print. It was a seed. And maybe, just maybe, it had found good soil.

I didn't need him to be where I was. I just wanted him to come a little closer.

Closer to the God who sees. Closer to the truth that had set me free.

And in that quiet moment, beside the man I love, watching him turn pages with curiosity and an open heart, I caught a glimpse of something I'd long prayed for.

Not loud or dramatic.
But real.
And beautiful.

Chapter Fifteen
THE CLOSENESS THAT SAVES

One afternoon, I pulled into the driveway after work. The day had been ordinary—nothing to hint at the news that was coming. As I turned off the engine, my phone rang.

I didn't recognise the number, but something nudged me to answer.

"Hello?"

"It's the hospital," the voice said. The hospital. The one I'd been waiting on for nine long years.

I froze.

"We're calling to let you know... your surgery is booked."

For a moment, I couldn't speak. Tears welled up in my eyes as the words sank in.

My heart whispered what my lips couldn't yet form: *It's finally happening.*

I'm going to be healed.

I sat there in the car, overwhelmed. Not just by the news—but by everything that had led to this point. The waiting. The pain. The unanswered questions.

And most of all, the way God had gently walked with me through every single step. This journey—especially the years since choosing to walk with Him—had taught me more than I ever imagined.

Each painful season had shaped me. Every delay had refined me. The brokenness had humbled me.

I thought back to who I was nine years ago. If I had known God like I do now, maybe I wouldn't have clung so tightly to bitterness, resentment, or despair. Maybe I would've found peace a little sooner.

But even in the waiting—even when I couldn't see it—God had never left me. He was there, holding me through it all.

And now, after all this time, my healing had come.

> "LORD my God, I called to you for help, and you healed me." — Psalm 30:2

That verse echoed through my heart like a gentle anthem.

I was reminded, yet again, that no matter how long the storm raged, God stayed.

He stayed when I couldn't pray. He stayed when I gave up hope. He stayed when I didn't understand why the healing was taking so long.

And the storm that once tried to break me? *It became the very storm that made me.* Or so I thought.

The surgery went well, and I was finally home recovering. It was Sabbath, and I found myself feeling low—disappointed that I couldn't be at church.

I lay curled on the lounge, surrounded by pillows and wrapped in a blanket, still a little foggy from the aftereffects of recovery. Then, a soft knock at the door surprised me.

Four familiar faces from church stood there. They had come to sing hymns, read Scripture, and pray for me—bringing a little bit of Church right into my home.

I was overwhelmed by their kindness.

One of the hymns they sang was *Be Still, My Soul*.

I still play it nearly every day. Its lyrics remind me to anchor myself in what's yet to come—God's promises, not just the pain of the moment.

"Yes, my soul, find rest in God; my hope comes from him. Truly he is my rock and my salvation; he is my fortress, I will not be shaken. My salvation and my honour depend on God; he is my mighty rock, my refuge. Trust in him at all times, you people; pour out your hearts to him, for God is our refuge." — Psalm 62:5-8

Though my physical recovery was progressing, I hadn't prepared for the mental toll.

I thought I would use my downtime productively, but I quickly sank into a state of restlessness.

I stayed in bed too long, lost all motivation, and found myself spiralling.

I had fallen out of rhythm—no morning routines, no Bible reading, no journaling, no prayers.

It all began to feel heavy. Hopeless.

Then, like a divine rescue mission, *Happy Holiday Club* arrived.

Remember the program I mentioned at the beginning of this book? A whole year had passed, and it was that time again.

Though I was still recovering, I was able to help in small ways—and it couldn't have come at a better time.

The program—restarted in 1997 by the Seventh-day Adventist Church—has introduced countless children to Jesus through the dedication of volunteers.

And this year, it helped restore me.

It was the nudge I needed to reconnect with God after feeling spiritually adrift.

I was assigned to guide a group of pre-teens as we explored different Bible stories.

I wasn't confident—definitely not as familiar with the stories as the others—*but I prayed.*

For the first time in what seemed like a long time, I prayed each morning for courage, wisdom, and that the kids would feel God's love through me. Through all of us.

By the last day, I felt proud of what I had done.

What once terrified me had become something I genuinely found joy in.

I could feel the Holy Spirit at work—growing me, stretching my comfort zones, and gently revealing that I'm capable of so much more with God than I ever imagined on my own.

> *"But the Advocate, the Holy Spirit, whom the Father will send in my name, will teach you all things and will remind you of everything I have said to you."*
> — John 14:26

I've always been the quiet type—shy, reserved, the kind of person who would rather observe from the edges than step into the spotlight.

In new or unfamiliar situations, I preferred to keep to myself.

Helping behind the scenes, in small ways, one-on-one, felt safe, manageable even.

But anything that required being upfront, speaking out loud, or—worse—performing in front of others! That was enough to make my stomach twist into anxious knots.

So, when my boss casually asked if I'd be willing to step in and voice a character for one of our *Jungle Tales* skits—an antelope named Dic-Dic—my instinctive reaction should have been a polite but firm *absolutely not*.

But somehow, before my mind had caught up with what was being asked, my mouth answered: *Yes*.

It took a moment for the reality of what I'd agreed to sink in. And when it did, fear came crashing in like a tidal wave.

I was trembling. My heart raced. I wanted to retreat, to undo my answer, to go back to what felt safe.

Instead, I found myself standing behind a screen, a microphone in front of me, and a printed script in my shaking hands.

My voice felt small, unsteady. Every muscle in my body was tense as I took a deep breath and read the first line:

"It's beautiful."

And strangely, it was.

Not just the scene or the line, but the moment itself.

Beautiful because I didn't run. Beautiful because something shifted inside me. Beautiful because, in the middle of my fear, I could feel God's presence.

I could feel the Holy Spirit giving me strength, not to perform perfectly, but to simply show up. To be brave in the small moment I'd been given.

That one moment turned into two.

I made it through that day and the next one as well.

Not because I suddenly became confident, but because I leaned into the One who was with me in my weakness.

It wasn't about sounding impressive or getting it all right. It was about saying yes even when I was afraid—and discovering that fear doesn't get to have the final word.

That belongs to faith.

And every time I remember that quiet, trembling yes, I'm reminded of what can happen when we stop listening to fear—and start trusting the Spirit who gives us courage to do things we never thought we could.

> *"For the Spirit God gave us does not make us timid, but gives us power, love and self-discipline."*
> *— 2 Timothy 1:7*

These were the moments when my heart felt like it could burst with gratitude—answers to prayer, a growing sense of God's presence. Those were the mountaintops: *bright, exhilarating, and almost surreal.*

But with every mountaintop, there is often a valley waiting below.

Joy and struggle seemed to walk hand in hand in this season, and I couldn't tell which one would stay longer.

It wasn't long after *Happy Holiday Club* that I found myself falling again—slipping back into the darkness I was sure I had left behind for good.

It came slowly at first, like a fog creeping in around the edges of my life. Then suddenly, it was everywhere.

That Sabbath, I didn't make it to church.

Instead, I spent the day waging a war in silence—a battle just to stay alive.

The weight pressing down on me was suffocating. I felt like I was drowning beneath it, grasping for something—*anything*—to hold onto, but coming up empty.

One day turned into two.

Two turned into more.

Hope faded, and I began to believe the lie that maybe I was too broken to ever really be free.

I wasn't praying. I wasn't reading. I wasn't reaching out.

I felt abandoned, even though deep down I knew God had never left me. But my thoughts were too loud, too chaotic, too dark.

His presence, which once felt so near, now seemed impossibly far.

Then came the drive.

I remember it vividly—the way the road curled along the outskirts of town, the silence in the car louder than words.

I wasn't going anywhere in particular... just looking. Searching for a tree. One strong enough, tall enough, fast enough to make the pain stop in an instant.

I passed tree after tree, my grip tightening on the steering wheel as tears streamed down my face.

My heart pounded with desperation. I was begging for release, aching for peace.

And yet, in the middle of all that anguish, I couldn't quite find the nerve to let go. I was mere moments away from a decision I could never undo.

Then, my phone lit up.

One message. Just four words.

Mum, I need you.

I stared at it, hands trembling, breath caught in my throat.

In that instant, everything stopped. It wasn't just a text. It was a lifeline. A whisper cutting through the storm. A divine interruption.

God had stepped in. Not with thunder or lightning or a voice from heaven—but with a simple, urgent reminder of who I was... and who I still had to live for.

It was the wake-up call I didn't even know I needed. Not because everything was instantly fixed or the darkness suddenly disappeared—but because, for the first time in days, I remembered I wasn't alone.

I remembered I had a purpose. I remembered that God still saw me, even in the valley. *Especially in the valley.*

That message saved my life.

And the God who orchestrated its timing reminded me that even when I can't see Him... even when I don't feel Him... *He is still there.*

He never stopped fighting for me—even when I had stopped fighting for myself.

"The thief comes only to steal and kill and destroy; I have come that they may have life, and have it to the full."
— John 10:10

I buried the darkness deep within me—ashamed, haunted by the weight of what almost was.

There was grief, not just over the pain I had felt, but over how close I had come to letting it consume me completely.

In the quiet that followed, I began to pray again. Whispers at first—fragile, uncertain. I asked for forgiveness. I thanked God for showing up when I couldn't see Him—for saving me when I had stopped reaching for Him.

But even in my gratitude, shame lingered.

I carried this unspoken belief that what I had done—what I had almost done—had put me beyond His favour.

How could I worship a holy God when I felt so unholy? How could I draw near when I wasn't sure He wanted me near?

That lie crept in slowly, but it stuck: *You're not worthy.*

Every time I opened my Bible or tried to sing in church, those words echoed in the back of my mind.

So I started to pull away—not because I didn't love God, but because I was convinced He couldn't love me the same way anymore. Shame distorted my view of Him, turning mercy into something I thought I had already exhausted.

I couldn't shake the question: *How could I have come so close to giving up... and still expect Him to welcome me back?*

I felt unworthy of His grace, unsure if I could ever stand in His presence again after walking so far from it.

A few Sabbaths later, my boss stood at the front of the church to preach.

Beforehand, he had casually asked me if I had any sermon topic ideas.

I didn't think much of it at the time, but I gave him a list—six off the top of my head that had been stirring in my heart lately: *Connection, Intentional Prayer, Healing, The Holy Spirit, Purpose, and Hope.*

Out of all the options, he chose *Connection.*

And as soon as he began to speak, I knew it wasn't a coincidence. It was God.

God knew exactly what my soul was aching for.

Not just surface-level encouragement, but a reminder that He was still reaching for me—even when I'd pulled away.

As my boss preached, the words struck deeper than I expected. They weren't just a sermon—they were a mirror. Each sentence felt like it was written for me. Spoken to me.

Because the truth was, I had drifted.

I had disconnected—from people, from prayer, from the very presence that had once carried me through my darkest nights.

I had let shame build a wall, and fear keep it standing.

But that Sabbath, brick by brick, those walls began to come down.

God wasn't scolding me. He wasn't condemning me.

He was gently calling me back—reminding me that *connection* with Him was never about me being perfect.

It was always about me being willing to return.

And in that moment, I started to look back.

To my surprise, partway through the sermon, I was called up once again to voice Dic-Dic the antelope in another *Jungle Tales* skit.

This time, the story hit differently.

Dic-Dic had fallen into a pit—a hunter's trap.

Relatable? Painfully.

Other animals tried to help, but none could.

Then Nhembo—the character who represented God—arrived. He called gently to Dic-Dic, inviting him to come closer so He could help.

It was the only way out. Dic-Dic chose to trust Him.

He kept his eyes fixed on Nhembo and, step by step, found his way out of the pit.

Nhembo then reassured him that they would journey together from that point on—and that staying close to Him was the safest way forward.

Staying close to Him—God—will always be the safest path.

Those words settled deep in my soul like a healing balm.

Because I was Dic-Dic. I knew what it felt like to fall. To be trapped in a place I couldn't escape on my own. To try everything—and still feel stuck.

But I also knew the gentle voice of God calling me closer.

And in that moment, He reminded me: *I wasn't alone in the pit.* I never was.

The safest way forward wasn't striving—*it was staying close to Him.*

> "I cling to you; your right hand upholds me."
> — Psalm 63:8

From that moment, I began to cling to God again—not just out of desperation, but with quiet determination.

I started praying more often, this time for myself. Mostly.

Desperate. Painful. Loud. Hard prayers.

That was new for me.

I had grown comfortable praying for others—for their healing, their strength, their direction—but turning that same compassion inward felt unfamiliar. Vulnerable. Almost selfish.

But I knew I needed Him. I needed His voice in the chaos.

It was clear that the heaviness had started creeping back in, like a shadow returning to a familiar place. I could feel myself near the edge of that deep, dark hole again.

So I prayed.

I asked God to guide me, to place someone safe in my path.

Someone I could trust. Someone I could speak to when I wasn't even sure what to say.

For days, I prayed without an answer.

Silence. Stillness. Waiting.

Then, seemingly out of nowhere, I felt a persistent tug toward one of the doctors I work with.

She wasn't my regular doctor, but she was a friend. A fellow believer. Kind. Steady.

The thought came gently but firmly: *Talk to her.*

So, I booked the appointment. Then I cancelled it. And rebooked. Then cancelled it again.

Three times I tried—and three times I pulled away.

Each time, I convinced myself I was okay. Or that someone else needed it more. Or that it was too late, too awkward, too soon to open up. I told myself I could handle it.

But God knew better.

That afternoon, after yet another cancelled slot—one I'd handed over to a walk-in patient—I was tidying up at the end of the day, mentally checking out.

And then I felt it: a gentle tap on my shoulder.

I turned, and there she was.

Her voice was soft, almost casual: *"Come with me."*

I hesitated. It was late. She should have been heading home.

But she waited. Patient. Kind.

So I followed her.

We walked down the quiet hallway, and as I sat down, hands trembling, pulling at my fingers, unsure how to begin.

She didn't rush me. She didn't prod.

She simply watched me with gentle eyes and a posture that said, *I'm here.*

And little by little, the words came.

The fear. The pain. The heaviness I'd been carrying.

I told her everything.

And as I spoke, it felt like a dam broke inside me—like bricks I didn't even know I was carrying were lifted, one by one, off my chest.

There were no easy fixes. No perfect solutions.

But there was relief.

When I walked out of her office, I felt something I hadn't felt in a long, long time: *free*.

God had not left me—not when I pushed Him away, not when I ignored the nudges, not even when I doubted He was still listening.

He had led me, patiently and persistently, to someone safe.

Someone who would listen without judgment and sit with me in the mess.

"The LORD himself goes before you and will be with you; he will never leave you nor forsake you. Do not be afraid; do not be discouraged." — Deuteronomy 31:8

I've learnt that closeness with God isn't about feeling Him all the time—it's about choosing to stay near, even in the silence.

Even in the storm.

Especially in the storm.

"The wounds we carry are not just scars, but gifts—equipping us to understand, empathise, and walk alongside others with compassion."

— FOUND

Chapter Sixteen

MIRACLES IN THE MESS

Working in a doctor's surgery in a small country town gave me a unique window into people's lives. It was more than just appointments and prescriptions—it was stories, struggles, hopes, and heartbreaks.

Over time, I got to know many patients—not just by name or condition, but by their very real-life journeys.

I always cared deeply about people—that's just part of who I am—but I never expected to get as emotionally involved as I did with one particular patient.

Sometimes, even when we try to keep professional boundaries, *the heart doesn't listen.*

This elderly man had become a regular visitor.

Over more than a year, I gradually learnt pieces of his life story—the battles he fought silently, the weight he carried each day.

He was quiet and kind, with a gentle strength that spoke of humility. Selfless in his actions and caring in his presence—*he carried a warmth that needed no words.*

I remember how he would sit patiently in my little room, sometimes lost in thought, other times sharing a small joke or a fleeting smile despite his obvious pain.

His gentleness struck me—how someone could bear such hardship and still offer kindness was a profound glimpse of grace in a hurting world.

Then one day, everything changed. His health deteriorated far more quickly than we could have imagined.

Within days, he slipped into unconsciousness. His doctor came to me quietly, with a seriousness that was impossible to ignore. I knew just by looking at her that it was just a matter of time. Any time. *The words hung heavy in the air.*

It was one of those moments where faith and reality collide—and the heart wrestles with the unbearable tension between hope and loss.

I remember vividly how I prayed—for him, for his family, for God's mercy. I prayed over and over, some prayers whispered with hope, others with fear.

I told myself to be ready for the worst, being okay that if God chose to take him, it would mean freedom from pain.

But I also clung tightly to hope.

Each day, I waited for news.

Each day, when it didn't arrive, I found a new reason to pray—to hope—to trust that God was still working a miracle.

One morning as I arrived at work, his doctor came rushing in, her face alight with joy. *"You won't believe it,"* she said breathlessly, *"but he's awake. And he's talking."*

I rushed to his bedside, heart pounding.

There he was—alive, smiling softly, just as gentle as ever.

"Hi sweetheart," he greeted me, like nothing had happened.

It was as though time had paused and the impossible had come to life.

Witnessing that moment felt like standing at the edge of a miracle—an unmistakable sign that God was at work, *even in the darkest valleys.*

Over the following days, he improved steadily, defying every expectation.

The day he was cleared to go home and water his lawn felt like a celebration—not just of health restored, but of hope renewed.

Such a simple act—watering a lawn—became a symbol of victory over death, pain, and despair.

This patient's journey reshaped how I prayed and how I saw God's hand in the messiness of life.

I learnt to pray with intention and consistency—not just in crisis, but daily—trusting God's plan even when answers didn't come quickly.

I also came to understand the emotional cost of caring for those on the edge of life and death.

In healthcare, loss is a constant visitor. While we cannot avoid the pain, God's grace offers healing and hope beyond it.

> "He performs wonders that cannot be fathomed, miracles that cannot be counted." – Job 9:10

It was around that time; I came across a powerful book called *Behind the Tears* by Dr. Bruce Robinson.

It explores suffering—not just the pain, but how we can survive it, learn from it, and transform it into something meaningful.

I wished I had read it earlier—during the seasons of pain, or when those I loved were hurting.

The book ministers not only to those suffering but also to those who stand beside them, caring and carrying burdens of their own.

One quote from the book has lingered in my heart:

> "Your wound is your gift." – Anonymous

What a beautiful and transformative way to see suffering.

The wounds we carry are not just scars, but gifts—equipping us to understand, empathise, and walk alongside others with compassion.

Through our pain, we become vessels of God's love—reflecting Jesus' heart in a world that desperately needs it.

> "We are therefore Christ's ambassadors, as though God were making his appeal through us. We implore you on Christ's behalf: Be reconciled to God."
> — 2 Corinthians 5:20

Becoming a Christian has been one of the most profound experiences of my life.

But I've come to realise that faith is not a one-time event—it's a lifelong journey.

The transition from living without Christ to walking in His light is filled with learning, struggles, and growth.

One of the most important lessons I've learnt is the power of community.

Being surrounded by other believers has been a *lifeline.*

Their encouragement, wisdom, and gentle support helped me navigate doubts and fears—and celebrate the small victories in faith.

When you're new to the Christian Walk, fellowship isn't just helpful—*it's essential.*

There is something indescribable about belonging to a community of believers.

You feel understood.

You feel accepted.

You feel loved.

It's a foretaste of heaven here on earth—a glimpse of the unity Jesus prayed for in John's Gospel.

> *"I have given them the glory that you gave me, that they may be one as we are one—I in them and you in me—so that they may be brought to complete unity. Then the world will know that you sent me and have loved them even as you have loved me."*
> *— John 17:22-23*

This unity, this connection, not only strengthens our faith, but it also serves as a powerful testimony of God's love to the world.

No matter how dark the path may seem, *we do not walk alone.*

The community of believers surrounds us, walking alongside us, pointing us back to Christ when we stray.

As I reflect on this chapter of my life, I am reminded that faith is a journey marked by miracles, trials, and growth.

God's presence sustains us through suffering.

God shapes our character through hardship.

God uses our wounds for His glory.

And the love and support of Christian fellowship provide strength and encouragement to keep walking—even when the path is steep and uncertain.

Wherever you find yourself on your journey, may you be encouraged to trust in God's miraculous power.

May you see the gift in your wounds.

And may you find strength in the loving community He provides.

"Depression doesn't knock before entering. It slips in quietly, inch by inch, until suddenly you realise you're already drowning."

— FOUND

Chapter Seventeen
LIGHTHOUSES IN THE STORM

It felt like I was only just beginning to understand what it meant to walk with God, let alone understand the deeper significance of something like baptism. It wasn't a conversation I heard around the dinner table or something I saw modelled growing up.

So when the thought of being baptised first stirred in my heart, I questioned it. Was I ready? Was this the right time? Shouldn't I have it all figured out first?

But as I wrestled with those doubts, I came to a quiet but powerful realisation—there is no such thing as a *"perfect time."*

Waiting for the stars to align or for myself to be perfectly prepared would only delay what my heart already longed for: *to publicly declare that I belonged to Jesus.*

I didn't have all the answers, but I had experienced enough of His grace to know I didn't want to walk without Him.

Baptism wasn't about having everything together—it was about surrender. And that could start now.

So somewhere along this unpredictable journey—through valleys of crushing doubt and mountaintops of fragile hope—I reached a place where I knew it was time.

Time to say yes.

Yes to God the Father.
Yes to His Son, Jesus Christ.
Yes to the Holy Spirit, who was quietly shaping me from the inside out.

Baptism is not just a public declaration, but a deeply personal moment where I gave God my whole heart and said, *"Yes, Lord. I'm Yours".*

I had been saved by grace, redeemed by Jesus' death on the cross, and now I wanted my life to be fully transformed by His Spirit.

But just as I set the date and prepared to step into those waters, the storm hit—harder than I ever imagined.

I thought I was doing better. I thought this would be another mountaintop moment. But there was one more valley waiting for me first.

I plunged into the depths of a mental and emotional breakdown—a wave that came fast and merciless.

That's the cruel nature of depression: *depression doesn't knock before entering. It slips in quietly, inch by inch, until suddenly you realise you're already drowning.*

That afternoon, I was gasping for breath through a flood of tears, my mind spiralling uncontrollably.

The chaos inside was deafening.

Somehow, I made it to my doctor. She sat with me for hours, speaking calm words into my chaos, gently reminding me I wasn't alone.

But I knew deep down—I had now reached the breaking point.

The mask of strength I'd been wearing cracked beyond repair. I was done pretending. I was broken. Desperate. Afraid of just how dark the night might get.

This time I didn't turn away from God, I cried out to Him for myself—not just for others—and I didn't stop.

For months, I whispered prayers like: *God, please, I don't want to feel like this anymore.*

Pleading that nothing good could come from it, that I didn't understand what He was doing. But heaven seemed silent.

When I was finally admitted to the hospital after battling terrifying suicidal thoughts, I felt abandoned — like maybe God had turned His face from me this time. For good.

Was I too far gone? Had He given up on me?

In my desperation, I was willing to accept help from anywhere — even agreeing to try therapy again, though I'd once vowed I never would.

Nervous and fragile, I joined my first telehealth session, only to wait 32 agonising minutes before realising no one was coming.

I felt crushed — crying out for help and being met with silence again.

The company apologised and promised to find me someone new. And a week later, they matched me with another psychologist.

Hesitant, uncertain if I could bear another disappointment, I whispered another quiet prayer: *God, please let this one show up.*

And he did.

That session became a turning point—a small one, as I began to see God's hand in the previous letdown.

We clicked immediately.

To my surprise, he was a Christian too—and that shared faith opened the door to the kind of therapy I desperately needed: *rooted in grace, understanding, and compassion.*

He listened—not just with his ears, but with his heart.

He helped me see my story from a new perspective and helped me understand why I was the way I was.

For the first time in a long while, I believed something good might grow from the darkness.

A mental health team formed around me. I connected with a case manager who became someone safe, someone whom I trusted and could turn to at any moment.

My psychiatrist adjusted medications with care.

And I began seeing a dietician, who helped me rebuild the basics—one small, hopeful step at a time.

Slowly, I realised that some of my battles weren't only emotional or spiritual—they were physical too.

I'd been so focused on surviving the storm that I'd neglected my body's cries for rest, nourishment, and water.

But God never separates the physical from the spiritual. Scripture reminds us that our bodies are temples of the Holy Spirit—worthy of care and honour.

> *"Do you not know that your bodies are temples of the Holy Spirit, who is in you, whom you have received from God? You are not your own; you were bought at a price. Therefore honour God with your bodies."*
> *— 1 Corinthians 6:19–20*

Jesus Himself modelled rest and restoration. Even He took time to eat, to withdraw, to be still.

It wasn't weakness—it was wisdom.

He knew we were created for rhythms of renewal, and that caring for our bodies is stewardship—not selfishness.

So I began to see sleep, nourishment, hydration—not as optional, but as sacred parts of my healing.

Living through this chapter was anything but straightforward. It was messy, raw, full of setbacks, tears, and silent battles no one else could see.

Nothing about it was easy. But one thing remained steady: *my faith.*

It wasn't always strong. It cracked. It wavered. Sometimes it was barely there at all. But it never disappeared.

Somehow, even when I couldn't hold on, God held on to me.

Even in my anger. Even when I felt abandoned. Even in my moments of deep doubt, I kept turning to Him.

My world had been flipped upside down.

Everything—family, work, daily functioning—was shaken. But my prayers became more honest, more raw, more real. *How can I be Your ambassador when I feel this broken?*

And slowly, I began to see: *my faith itself was the blessing.* Fragile as it was, it endured.

It wasn't my strength holding me—it was God's. His steady hand kept me here. And the peace I longed for? It came—not because circumstances changed, but because He was with me in the midst of it all.

My safe place. My rest. My anchor. My lighthouse.

In my first breakdown, back in 2019, I referred to the people helping me as *"lifelines."* This time, a new image formed in my heart: I was a ship tossed in a violent storm, with no compass, no GPS—just a flicker of light on the horizon. *A lighthouse.*

Lighthouses don't calm the storm. They don't stop the waves. But they show you where the shore is. They help you keep going.

I started noticing my own lighthouses—those gentle guides back to hope:

Scripture, grounding me in truth when everything else felt like a lie.

Prayer, a place to pour out my heart and find solid ground again.

Friends who showed up, who checked in without judgment.

Worship music that soothed my aching spirit.

A kind word from a stranger when I least expected it.

A perfectly timed text message that felt like a hug.

Even the sunrise after a night too dark to sleep.

But above all, *God was the greatest lighthouse*—constant, unwavering.

"He has saved us and called us to a holy life—not because of anything we have done but because of his own purpose and grace. This grace was given us in Christ Jesus before the beginning of time."
— 2 Timothy 1:9

I thought often of the story in Matthew 8—the disciples, terrified, panicking in the boat while the storm raged.

Jesus was with them, asleep—peace itself in their chaos. With one word, He calmed the wind and the waves.

"He replied, 'You of little faith, why are you so afraid?' Then he got up and rebuked the winds and the waves, and it was completely calm."
— Matthew 8:26

That story reminded me: the storm may rage on, but God is in it with me. Always.

I leaned deeper into prayer—not polished or perfect, just raw and honest.

And I realised something profound: peace doesn't come from the absence of pain—it comes from the presence of God.

The more I opened the Bible, the more verses felt like lifeboats—keeping my head above water:

"Your word is a lamp for my feet, a light on my path." —
Psalm 119:105

"Let us then approach God's throne of grace with confidence, so that we may receive mercy and find grace to help us in our time of need."
— Hebrews 4:16

Prayer became more than a routine. It became my rhythm, my refuge.

But trusting God through the storm wasn't easy. Especially when mental health struggles made everything foggy and uncertain.

I had to choose—again and again—to believe He was guiding me, even when I couldn't see the way.

Hebrews 4:16 reminded me I could come as I was—boldly, confidently, even broken.

When God doesn't answer the way we expect, it's not rejection. It's often an invitation.

Like Paul with his thorn, sometimes God doesn't remove the pain—He gives grace to endure it and strength to walk through it.

Paul's thorn drew him into deeper intimacy with God.

Maybe mine would, too. Maybe this storm was preparing me for baptism.

My relationship with God had never been more personal, more raw, more real. I was learning to lean. To trust. To surrender. Every day, over and over.

So I kept praying. Kept opening His Word. Kept seeking the lighthouses He placed around me.

Mental health is scary. It's isolating. And while it's being talked about more, too many still suffer alone, silently.

That stirred something inside me.

I prayed, *God, show me how to use this pain for purpose.*

As I waited, I began learning. Reading. Researching.

Slowly, He revealed the next steps.

I felt a new calling stir—*to be a lighthouse for someone else.*

I'm not saying I have it all figured out. Healing isn't linear. But I am getting better.

I've found joy again—in small things. I've picked up old hobbies.

I've laughed more. I've rested more. I've waited more.

And time and again, I've seen God gently lead me back to shore.

And my baptism? *It's just around the corner.*

I may have walked through another storm. But this time, I knew where to look.

I had my lighthouses. I had my faith.

And above all—I had the God who calms the wind and waves.

He didn't let go of me. Not once.

"I was lowered beneath. I was raised to a new life. And just like that—I was marked forever. A follower of Jesus. A daughter of the King. A new creation."

— FOUND

Chapter Eighteen
THE DAY I SAID YES

Before I knew it, the day of my baptism had arrived.

It looked like any other Sabbath in our little country church—Julia's fingers dancing across the piano keys, filling the room with familiar sounds; warm, friendly faces offering smiles of encouragement and joy.

But something felt different. The pews were fuller than usual. My little family were there, and friends had come from near and far, gathering to witness this sacred moment.

Pastor T opened the service with words that grounded the occasion in profound truth.

He spoke of baptism not as a mere ritual, but as a deeply symbolic and sacred act—one of commitment, surrender, and spiritual rebirth.

"It's not magic water" he reminded us, and went on to reassure us that baptism is not a reset button that guarantees a life without trials.

Baptism is about dying to our old selves, being cleansed by grace, and rising to new life in Christ. It's about a heart turned toward Heaven.

I was especially grateful he said that. My daughter, Emileigh, had been viewing baptism almost like a fairy tale—believing that you come out of the water completely changed and flawless. It was important for everyone to hear: baptism is not the end of our struggles.

It is the beginning of a walk with Jesus, where we are never alone again.

I had carefully chosen the music for the day—songs that told the story of my heart and journey:

The Old Rugged Cross, to remember what Jesus did for me.

Open the Eyes of My Heart, a prayer for deeper spiritual vision.

Amazing Grace, because what better anthem is there for a life rescued by love?

There Was Jesus, a powerful reminder that He's been with me all along.

And finally, *Goodness of God*, because I will sing of His faithfulness all my days.

During the service, Pastor T reminded us that faith is exactly that—a journey. It's not a single step or event, but a daily turning of the heart toward God, a daily surrender to His will.

He spoke of the Father who runs toward His children with open arms—a story I had longed to believe. The story of the Prodigal Son hit me deeply. I never really had that kind of father growing up. But now, I have one—my Heavenly Father. A Father who pursues, who loves relentlessly, who runs to meet me when I turn back home.

That's what baptism is: *turning around, coming home, letting the Father embrace you.*

As the service continued, my nerves bubbled up inside me. It was almost time to stand and share my testimony.

As I have mentioned before, I've never liked being the centre of attention, and I've always avoided the spotlight.

But when I stood, trembling and shaky, my heart pounding, the words came flowing out—because they were true, because the Holy Spirit was right there with me.

My Testimony

"For I can do everything through Christ who gives me strength." – Philippians 4:13

I was immediately drawn to this verse as I scrolled through Scripture at the very start of my journey, one reason being that strength is something that I have felt I have lacked since a small girl. It is only through Jesus's strength that I am standing here in front of you all today.

I am a bundle of nerves squirming endlessly whenever I have to get up in front of anyone, but since coming to know God those nerves seem not to last as long. I thank God for that—without Him I wouldn't be standing here at all.

The second thing I was drawn to was the 4 and 13, my two favourite numbers. And yes, I have looked at all the 4:13 and 13:4 verses in every book of the Bible.

Let me take you back to the very beginning of how I ended up standing here today.

It has been 716 days since someone told me that I should pick up a Bible. I went home and downloaded it on my phone, and I explored it briefly, but it was tough to understand. Thankfully, I had some guidance from others—one being the same person who told me to pick up the Bible.

It has been 617 days since that same person invited me to church, Sabbath School in particular, as I had told him how much fun Emileigh had at Happy Holiday Club.

If you haven't already guessed, I love numbers.

497 days ago, I was in this church on Sabbath, crying, as I was surrounded by so much love and kindness as those around me prayed for my husband Chris, who was facing another cancer scare.

I was completely blanketed in comfort as tears ran down my face, realising the awe of God. I have no doubt the Holy Spirit was working in everyone there that day.

When I got home, I surrendered all my fear and worries to Him. I left it all in God's hands.

This particular day is what I look back on as my conversion. I cannot even describe the feeling I had when this happened.

So today is the first day I publicly declare that Jesus is my Saviour, that He has saved me, that I am chosen.

And as I partake in this baptism, you are all witnesses to what God has done for me.

He picked me up, He turned me around, He placed my feet on solid ground—a couple of lines out of one of my many praise songs.

Holding back tears, I continued:

This journey has not been easy. Becoming a Christian is not a walk in the park.

But why walk alone in this earthly world, when I can choose to walk with God?

Even when I fall to a heap, He doesn't just keep walking, leaving me there—*He carries me.*

I cannot tell you how much my life has changed. My desires and values have changed.

I love learning more and more from the Bible and knowing God's truth, and that it is only through His unconditional love for us that we are saved.

When you read about Jesus's baptism in Matthew 3:13–17 it says:

"Then Jesus came from Galilee to the Jordan to be baptised by John. But John tried to deter him, saying, 'I need to be baptised by you, and do you come to me?' Jesus

replied, 'Let it be so now; it is proper for us to do this to fulfil all righteousness.' Then John consented. As soon as Jesus was baptised, he went up out of the water. At that moment heaven was opened, and he saw the Spirit of God descending like a dove and alighting on him. And a voice from heaven said, 'This is my Son, whom I love; with him I am well pleased.'"

And this is why, as a disciple of Jesus and as a new believer, I choose to follow wherever He leads—including into the waters of baptism.

Lastly, I expressed my profound gratitude to everyone who had walked beside me on this journey.

The love, support, and encouragement have meant more than words can say.

My baptism was more than just a symbolic moment—it's the beginning of a new chapter in my life.

A chapter where I boldly and publicly declare:

Jesus is my Saviour. My Protector. My Comforter.

And above all, I thanked God—who gave me life, led me here to this little country town, and gifted me the greatest blessing of all: *life with Him.*

As I closed my testimony, tears threatened to spill over. My heart pounded again, but this time it was joy.

I stepped away and headed to the changing area.

Surrounded by my family, my church family and friends—each a piece of this beautiful story God is writing in my life.

I entered the baptismal font.

I was lowered beneath. I was raised to a new life. And just like that—I was marked forever. A follower of Jesus. A daughter of the King. A new creation.

The water was warm. The Spirit was stronger.

> "We were therefore buried with him through baptism into death in order that, just as Christ was raised from the dead through the glory of the Father, we too may live a new life." — Romans 6:4

This is my new life

This is the beginning of forever.

Epilogue: A Story Still Being Written

I never set out to write from a place of healing.
I started writing because I didn't know how else to survive.

Some people retreat.
Some cry.
Some run.
I wrote.

I wrote in journals I never intended to share—scribbling through tears at midnight, typing prayers I didn't know were prayers.

Not polished. Not poetic. Just honest.

At first, it was just me and God.
Me—emptying the ache.
God—meeting me in every word.

That's the strange beauty of writing from the middle of healing:

You don't wait until you're whole.
You just begin—shaky, raw, willing.
And that's where God meets you.

This book was never meant to be a book at the beginning.

It started as scattered pieces of my heart, stories I wasn't sure I'd ever share, moments I lived through with trembling faith and just enough strength to whisper, *"God, help me".*

Finishing it has been one of the hardest things I've ever done.

Not because I ran out of words—but because it meant going back. Back to the places that still sting, to the memories I carry tenderly.

But it also meant seeing how far God has brought me. Tracing His fingerprints through every page. Remembering, with certainty:

He was there.
He is here.
And He's not finished yet.

Writing this book became part of my healing.

Sharing it—well, that's the *surrender.*

Because it feels vulnerable—like handing someone your journal and hoping they find something that breathes life.

But I didn't write to impress.
I wrote to reach.
Even just one.

If something in these pages made you pause, breathe, or pray—*it was worth it.*

My deepest hope is this:
That someone drowning in the middle of their story feels less alone.
That someone who wonders if God is listening will remember—He never left.
That someone unsure where to begin will see that healing doesn't have to be perfect. *It just has to start.*

You don't need to have it all figured out to come to Jesus. You just need to come.
You don't need the right words to pray. You just need to speak.
You don't need to be whole to be loved. You already are.

I didn't grow up knowing God.
I didn't know the Bible.
I didn't even know if I believed He was real.

But one conversation about faith cracked something open in me.

What began as a spark became a slow, steady flame—not through a dramatic moment, but through ordinary days, gentle nudges, unexpected peace, and timely words I couldn't explain.

This book captures about eighteen months of that journey of discovering, wrestling, surrendering, learning, and growing.

It's not the story of someone who's arrived, but of someone still walking—slowly, faithfully, sometimes wearily—toward the One who found her.

Each page bears the marks of change:
not all at once, but moment by moment—through Scripture, through prayer, through community, through tears, and through quiet victories that only God and I will ever fully understand.

Following Jesus hasn't removed every struggle—but it's given me a Shepherd who walks with me, a Father who holds me, a Savior who understands me, and a Spirit who strengthens me.

That truth anchors me now.

And my purpose—the one God continues to reveal—is to share Jesus through words.

Not because I have all the answers, but because I've seen what happens when He steps into a life that didn't even know He was there.

So, if you've made it to this page, my hope is simple:
That something here drew you closer to Him.
Even if it was just one moment.
One story.
One verse.
One breath of hope.

Because this isn't just my story—it's a reminder that you have one too.

And God is writing it. Even now.

You don't have to wait to be whole.
You don't have to have it all together.
You just have to open the door.

God is faithful.

He is still in the business of finding the lost. I know that now—because I was one of them.

And now, I am found.

About the Author

Tanya Leigh Wood is a wife, mother of four, and writer who never grew up knowing God—and certainly never imagined she'd write a book about Him.

Tanya writes from the heart—with raw honesty and heartfelt conviction—about what it means to be found by a God she now cannot live without. Through every chapter of her life, she shares how Jesus meets us in our pain, our questions, and our everyday moments with grace that both surprises and sustains.

Now living in a small country town in Western Australia with her husband and children, Tanya is passionate about helping others who feel lost, broken, or unworthy to see that they are never too far gone for God. Her greatest joy is using words to point people to the One who found her—so they, too, might discover they have been seen, loved, and pursued all along.

REFERENCES

Note: the following sources were referenced or mentioned throughout this book for reflection, learning, or inspiration.

BOOKS

Bruce Robinson, Behind the Tears: Understanding, Surviving and Growing from Suffering. Perth, WA: The University of Western Australia Press, 2013.

Lee Strobel, The Case for Christ: A Journalist's Personal Investigation of the Evidence for Jesus. Grand Rapids, MI: Zondervan, 1998.

Lee Strobel, with Rob Suggs. The Case for Christ for Kids. Grand Rapids, MI: Zonderkidz, 2006.

Ellen G. White, Patriarchs and Prophets, p. 48. Mountain View, CA: Pacific Press Publishing Association, 1890.

Ellen G. White, The Ministry of Healing, p. 470. Mountain View, CA: Pacific Press Publishing Association, 1905.

Vaughan Roberts, God's Big Picture: A Bible Overview. Nottingham, UK: Inter-Varsity Press, 2002.

Greg Budd, One Miracle After Another: The Pavel Goia Story. Hagerstown, MD: Review and Herald Publishing Association, 2013.

Paul White, Jungle Doctor's Fables. Grand Rapids: Moody Press, various years.

SONGS

"Be Still, My Soul." Seventh-day Adventist Hymnal, no. 461. Lyrics by Katharina von Schlegel, trans. Jane Borthwick. Music by Jean Sibelius. Public domain.

"Amazing Grace." Seventh-day Adventist Hymnal, no. 108. Lyrics by John Newton. Public domain.

"The Old Rugged Cross." Seventh-day Adventist Hymnal, no. 159. Lyrics and music by George Bennard. Public domain.

"Open the Eyes of My Heart." Written by Paul Baloche. © 1997 Integrity's Hosanna! Music. Performed by 7 Hills Worship.

"There Was Jesus." Written by Casey Beathard, Jonathan Smith, and Zach Williams. © 2019 Provident Label Group LLC. Performed by CAIN.

"Goodness of God." Written by Ben Fielding, Ed Cash, Jason Ingram, Jenn Johnson, and Brian Johnson. © 2018 Bethel Music Publishing/Alletrop Music. Performed by CeCe Winans.

"I Surrender." Written by Leslie Jordan and David Leonard. © 2011 Integrity's Alleluia! Music/Integrity Worship Music. Performed by All Sons & Daughters.

"I'm So Blessed." Written by Logan Cain, Madison Cain, Taylor Cain, Jonathan Smith, and Matthew West. © 2022 Provident Label Group LLC. Performed by CAIN.

VIDEOS & MEDIA

Pastor Pavel Goia, Sermons, WA Seventh-day Adventist Easter Camp, 2023. www.youtube.com/@AdventistsWA

The Case for Christ, directed by Jon Gunn. Pure Flix, 2017.

"Give Me an Answer" – Series by Pastor Cliffe Knechtle, YouTube. www.youtube.com/@givemeananswer

The Bible (TV Miniseries). Created by Mark Burnett and Roma Downey. Directed by Crispin Reece, Tony

Mitchell, and Christopher Spencer. Aired on The History Channel, 2013. Distributed by 20th Century Fox Home Entertainment.

APPS & TOOLS

YouVersion Bible App, Life.Church. www.youversion.com

"A Teen's Guide to: Knowing Who God Is." Written by Tonia Gutting for the Hero Squad Program of the American Bible Society. Available on the YouVersion Bible App. © American Bible Society. https://www.americanbible.org/ http://www.myherosquad.org Accessed via https://www.youversion.com

"Fruit of the Spirit." Bible reading plan by GlobalRize. Available on the YouVersion Bible App. © GlobalRize. https://www.globalrize.org/ Accessed via https://www.youversion.com

"Healed by Jesus." Bible reading plan by YouVersion. Available on the YouVersion Bible App. © Life.Church. Accessed via https://www.youversion.com

Koorong Christian Bookstore. www.koorong.com

Appendix: Scripture References

These verses are the spiritual thread throughout the story—reminders of God's presence, promises, and purpose. Each one was chosen with intention and speaks into different moments of discovery, healing, and surrender.

Old Testament

Genesis 2:18 – God created us for community and companionship.

Exodus 20:8 – A call to rest, reflect, and connect with God.

Deuteronomy 31:8 – Assurance that God is always with us.

Job 9:10 – A reminder to trust God in every season.

Psalm 9:10 – A reminder to trust God in every season.

Psalm 18:30 – God's ways are trustworthy and true.

Psalm 30:2 – A testimony of answered prayer and healing.

Psalm 34:8 – An invitation to experience God's goodness.

Psalm 40:2 – A powerful image of rescue and redemption.

Psalm 62:5-8 – A reminder of God as our refuge.

Psalm 63:8 – God holds us in our weakness and need.

Psalm 66:16 – An invitation to hear and share God's goodness.

Psalm 77:11 – Encouragement to recall God's past faithfulness.

Psalm 95:1-2 – A joyful invitation to praise and thank God.

Psalm 119:105 – God's Word gives direction and clarity.

Psalm 130:5 – A call to patient trust in God's timing.

Proverbs 11:25 – Generosity blesses both the giver and receiver.

Proverbs 16:9 – God directs our steps even when we don't see it.

Isaiah 47:14 – A warning about trusting in anything but God.

Jeremiah 17:14 – A cry for healing and restoration.

Jeremiah 29:13 – God promises to be found by the seeking heart.

Zephaniah 3:17 – A beautiful image of God's delight in us.

New Testament

Gospels

Matthew 2:16 – A reflection on suffering and injustice.

Matthew 3:13-17 – An example of obedience and the Father's affirmation.

Matthew 5:16 – Shine your light to honour God.

Matthew 6:9-10 – Jesus' model for how we should pray.

Matthew 7:7 – God responds to those who earnestly seek Him.

Matthew 7:8 – A promise that God is always in reach for the sincere seeker.

Matthew 8:26 – Jesus brings peace even in the middle of chaos.

Matthew 10:38 – A call to sacrifice and full surrender.

Matthew 18:19-20 – God is present in community and united prayer.

Matthew 19:26 – Nothing is impossible with God.

Matthew 26:28 – A picture of Christ's sacrifice for our salvation.

Mark 5:28 – A powerful moment of faith and hope.

Mark 5:34 – Jesus responds to faith with compassion.

Mark 12:29-31 – The greatest commandments summed up.

Luke 6:28 – A radical call to love even enemies.

Luke 24:45 – Jesus helps us grasp spiritual truth.

Luke 24:51-52 – Christ's return to heaven and the disciples' joy.

John 3:16 – The central message of the Gospel.

John 6:40 – Hope for the future through faith in Christ.

John 6:48 – Jesus alone satisfies our deepest needs.

John 8:7 – A challenge to show mercy and self-awareness.

John 8:10-11 – Grace and restoration offered to the broken.

John 9:3 – Purpose in suffering.

John 10:10 – Jesus offers true and abundant life.

John 14:26 – A promise of guidance and truth.

John 15:4 – Spiritual growth comes from abiding in Jesus.

John 16:7 – Jesus promises the Holy Spirit.

John 16:33 – Jesus has overcome.

John 17:22-23 – Jesus' prayer for unity among believers.

John 19:30 – It is finished. The final words of Christ—our salvation completed.

Acts and Letters

Acts 1:8 – Empowerment to live and witness boldly.

Romans 6:4 – A symbol of dying to self and rising in Christ.

Romans 6:23 – The gift of God is eternal life.

Romans 8:26 – When we can't pray, He intercedes for us.

Romans 10:14 – A call to share the Gospel boldly.

1 Corinthians 6:19-20 – Live in a way that honours God.

1 Corinthians 7:10 – Instructions on relationships and commitment.

2 Corinthians 5:17 – A declaration of transformed identity.

2 Corinthians 5:20 – We are Christ's ambassadors.

Galatians 5:22-23 – The fruit of the Spirit.

Ephesians 6:10-11 – Spiritual protection in life's battles.

Philippians 2:3 – Live with humility, valuing others above yourself.

Philippians 4:13 – God's strength enables us.

Philippians 4:19 – God provides abundantly and faithfully.

2 Timothy 1:7 – God gives courage and self-discipline.

2 Timothy 1:9 – God's purpose is bigger than our past.

Hebrews 4:16 – We can come to Him boldly in prayer.

Hebrews 10:24-25 – Never stop encouraging and gathering with others.

Hebrews 11:1 – Faith means trusting the unseen.

1 Peter 3:8 – A call to live united in love and humility.

1 John 3:1 – We are His beloved children.

1 John 4:7-8 – Love is the core of who God is.

1 John 4:16 – God is love. Living in love means living in God.

Revelation 12:9 – A reminder of the enemy—but also his defeat.

Reflection Invitation

As you've read through these Scriptures woven into each chapter of **FOUND**, I invite you to go back and sit with them slowly. Let them speak to you. Let them anchor you. These words aren't just for the pages of a book—they are the living breath of God, meant to transform, restore, and guide your journey.

May they light your path, steady your soul, and remind you—*you are seen, you are loved, and you are never alone.*

www.ingramcontent.com/pod-product-compliance
Lightning Source LLC
Chambersburg PA
CBHW071235070526
44583CB00017B/2190